THE CRIME OF THE CALF

An Exposition of Exodus, Chapter 32

According To The Mysteries

4th Edition

For My Parents, Louis & Evelyn Goldstein
Who Did Their Best For Me
and
For Aunt Miriam

4th Edition
June 2015

© Copyright 2015 by Christ-Centered Kabbalah

All rights reserved.

Published @ Long Island, NY June 2015

ISBN-13: 978-0692243817
ISBN-10: 069224381X

Alternate Translation Bible (ATB)©

Sheila R. Vitale, Translator

Comments by Sheila R. Vitale

No part of this book may be reproduced, in any form, without written permission from the publisher

Requests for permission to reproduce selections from this book should be mailed to:

Christ-Centered Kabbalah

P O Box 562

Port Jefferson Station, NY 11776-0562

(631) 331-1493

Christ-Centered Kabbalah
~ The Compleat Kabbalah ~
Sheila R. Vitale
Pastor, Teacher & Founder

Ministry Staff
Jesse Aldrich, Elder (McGregor, MN)
Sandra L. Aldrich, Elder (McGregor, MN)
Margaret Mobolaji-Lawal, Elder (Lagos, Nigeria)

Administrative Staff
Susan Panebianco, Office Manager

Technical Staff
Lape Mobolaji-Lawal, Database Administrator
Brooke Paige, Software Specialist
Dele Adegbite, MP3 Manager
June Eble, Shipping Manager
Rita L. Rora, FTP Manager

Ministry Illustrators
Cecilia H. Bryant (Oct. 18, 1921 – Oct. 23, 2013)
Fidelis Onwubueke

Music Staff
June Eble, Singer, Lyricist and Clarinetist
Don Gervais, Singer, Lyricist and Guitarist
Rita L. Rora, Singer, Lyricist and Guitarist

TABLE OF AUTHORITIES

1. **Brown Driver & Briggs' Hebrew Lexicon**, Woodside Bible Fellowship, Ontario, Canada, Licensed From The Institute for Creation Research.

2. **Englishman's Greek-Hebrew Concordance.**

3. **Gesenius' Hebrew and Chaldee Lexicon to the Old Testament** Scriptures, Baker Book House, Grand Rapids, Michigan.

4. **The Interlinear Bible** (Jay P. Green, Sr.), Hendrickson Publisher's, Peabody, Massachusetts 01961-3473.

5. **The Interlinear Bible (transliterated), Biblesoft and International Bible Translators, Inc.**

6. **Nave's Topical Bible.**

7. **Nelson's Bible Dictionary**, Thomas Nelson, Inc., Publishers, Nashville, Tennessee.

8. **Strong's Exhaustive Concordance** (James Strong) Thomas Nelson, Inc., Publishers, Nashville, Tennessee.

9. **Strong's Hebrew And Chaldee Dictionary** (James Strong), Thomas Nelson, Inc., Publishers, Nashville, Tennessee.

10. **Strong's Greek Dictionary** (James Strong), Thomas Nelson, Inc., Publishers, Nashville, Tennessee.

11. **The New Thayer's Greek-English Lexicon Of The New Testament**, Hendrickson Publisher's, Peabody, Massachusetts 01961-3473.

12. **Unger's Bible Dictionary** (Merrill F. Unger), The Moody Bible Institute of Chicago, Chicago, Illinois 60610.

13. **1979 Authorized Version** (AV), The On-Line Bible

14. **Stephanus Greek Text**, The On-Line Bible

15. **Green's Literal Translation**, The On-Line Bible

TABLE OF CONTENTS

Preface i
  Why Another Translation? i
  Preparing To Translate................................. iii
  Alternate Translations Are Progressive iv
  The Torah (The Word of God) Is Alive iv

Exodus, Chapter 32... ix
  King James Version ix
  Alternate, Amplified Translation xv
    Fear Of Abandonment................................... A
    Emotional & Spiritual Weakness .... A
    A New Nature .... B
    Spiritual Sacrifices .... B
    Aaron Mocked... C
    Pharaoh's Neck .... D
    Completed Personalities................................E
    Blind To Sin ....E
    Jehovah's Promise..F
    Reprieve ....F
    A Spiritual Mind .... G
    Engraved By God.. G
    Sin Recognized... G
    The Second Witness .... H
    Inclined To Do Evil..................................... H
    Bound To Pharaoh...I
    Widowhood I
    A Great Sin...I
    Power For Themselves I
    Moses Intercedes .... J
    Sowing & Reaping .... J

 Priests Challenged .... J
 Mortal Men Challenged .... K
 Seized & Slain .... K
 The Female Power Burned L
 Seed & Water L
 Jehovah Is God L
The 1st Sin .... O
Idolatry For Leaders .... O
 Idolatry 1
 Fear Of Abandonment 1
Emotional & Spiritual Weakness 2

Aaron Judges 3

The 1st Sin 3

Deliverance From 3
Fear Of Abandonment 3
Abel's Blood Guilt 5
 A New Nature 7
 Spiritual Sacrifices 9

Exodus 32:7-10 12

The 2nd Sin 13

Self-Appointed 13
Authority 13
 Aaron Mocked 15

The 3rd Sin 19

Illegal Acquisition Of 19
Spiritual Power 19
 Pharaoh's Neck 21
 Completed Personalities 22

Exodus 32:11-14 23

 Blind To Sin 25

An Immortal Body 27

    Jehovah's Promise 29
    Reprieve 30

Exodus 32:15-18 33
A Spiritual Mind 35
Engraved By God 36

Moses Judges 39

The 2nd Sin 39

Deliverance from Fear 39
Of Authority 39
    Sin Recognized 41
    The Second Witness 41

Exodus 32:21-25 43
    Inclined To Do Evil 45

Moses Judges The 3rd Sin 47

Deliverance From 47
Fear of Pharaoh 47
    Bound To Pharaoh 49
    Widowhood 49

Exodus 32:30-35 51
    A Great Sin 53
    Power For Themselves 53
    Moses Intercedes 54

Hunger 57

For Jehovah's Words 57
    Sowing & Reaping 59

Exodus 32:26-29 61

Moses' Prayer 63
Two Opinions 67
    Priests Challenged 69
Jehovah's Fire 71

Mortal Men Challenged 73
Baal's Silence.. 75
Seized & Slain 79

Exodus 32:19-20, 29 81

The Female Power Burned... 83
Seed & Water 87
Jehovah Is God... 91

Exodus, Chapter 32 95

Alternate Translation.. 95
Fear Of Abandonment 95
Emotional & Spiritual Weakness 95
A New Nature 96
Spiritual Sacrifices 97
Aaron Mocked.. 97
Pharaoh's Neck 98
Completed Personalities 99
Blind To Sin 99
Jehovah's Promise.. 100
Reprieve 100
A Spiritual Mind 101
Engraved By God 101
Sin Recognized.. 102
The Second Witness 102
Inclined To Do Evil... 102
Bound To Pharaoh... 103
Widowhood 103
A Great Sin.. 103
Power For Themselves 104
Moses Intercedes 104
Sowing & Reaping 105
Priests Challenged 105
Mortal Men Challenged 105
Seized & Slain.. 106
Female Power Burned..................................... 106
Seed & Water 107
Jehovah Is God.. 107

Footnotes Appendix 109
Reference 239
Footnotes 241
   Table Of Notes 241
      Sorted By Note Number 241
      Sorted By Scripture 245
      Sorted By Title 251

Soncino Zohar 257
Appendices 259
   The 10 Sefirot 261
   The Keter 262
   Five Levels Of Soul 263
   Soul Universes 264

About The Author 273

The Alternate Translation Bible©

The Alternate Translation Bible (ATB) is an original translation of the Scripture.

Alternate Translation of the Old Testament©
Alternate Translation, Exodus, Chapter 32 (Crime of the Calf)©
Alternate Translation, Daniel, Chapter 8©
Alternate Translation, Daniel, Chapter 11©

Alternate Translation of the New Testament©
Alternate Translation, 2 Thessalonians, Chapter 2 (Sophia)©
Alternate Translation, 1st John, Chapter 5©
Alternate Translation, the Book of Colossians
    (To The Church At Colosse)
Alternate Translation, the Book of Corinthians, Chapter 11
    (Corinthian Confusion)
Alternate Translation, the Book of Jude (The Common Salvation)©

Alternate Translation of the Book of the Revelation of Jesus Christ
    to St. John©
Traducción Alternada del Libro de Revelación de Jesucristo©

For Additional Information, please contact:

Christ-Centered Kabbalah
Sheila R. Vitale
PO Box 562
Port Jefferson Station, NY 11776 USA

_____

Exodus, Chapter 32

An Exposition
According To The Mysteries

Rev 10:7

⁷But in the days of the voice of the seventh angel, when he shall begin to sound, the mystery of God should be finished, as he hath declared to his servants the prophets.

KJV

Preface

Why Another Translation?

The King James Translators were not spiritual men. They were scholars who, themselves, perceived the Deity of the Scripture as an unforgiving, punishing God. But there is another Message, a spiritual understanding of the Scripture called *the Doctrine of Christ*, which reveals a loving God, whose sole intention towards mankind is to deliver us from destruction and death.

There are many definitions for each word in the English dictionary, and many translations for each Hebrew and Greek word in the original text of the Scripture.

The King James Translators dealt with the problem of one Hebrew source word appearing several times in a single Chapter, by using a different English word each time that the Hebrew word appears. The English word choices of the translator, then, are directly related to 1) his knowledge of the Word of God, 2) the degree to which he is influenced by the Spirit of Revelation and 3) the accepted understanding of the Word of God at the time.

The Spirit of Revelation influences the translator to choose legitimate *Alternate Translations* from the Hebrew and Greek lexicons listed in the front of *The Prophecies of Daniel According to Kabbalah, Chapter 8, Alternate Translation*, to express the spiritual intent of the Scripture. The Alternate English Translations for some of the Hebrew words in the Scripture are just as legitimate as the choices made by the King James Translators, but they render a radically different, and much more positive Translation than the Authorized Version.

Multiple English translations for the same Hebrew word in the King James text are perfectly legitimate examples of Translator's License, and simply prove our point: *The King James Translators, themselves, used multiple definitions of the same Hebrew Word.*

The Prophecies of Daniel According to Kabbalah, Chapter 8, is a Spiritual Translation of the Scripture, which is as legitimate to the Spiritual Mind, as the King James translation is to the Carnal Mind. The *Alternate Translation Bi*ble sounds radically different than the King James and other translations, because it must be Spiritually Discerned (1 Cor. 2:14).

A knowledge of the True Intent of the author of the Scripture, and a desire to understand the message that he intended to convey, should be the top priority for all genuine seekers of *Truth*.

God is the Living Word that feeds Mankind through imperfect vessels. Beware of idolatry for the King James, or any other Translation, because *all translations* are the work of imperfect, mortal men. Seek God and He will direct your paths (Pro. 3:6).

May the Spirit of Truth expose all of our wrong thinking, and may the Truth intended by the author of the Word cleave to our heart and mind, because the Spirit of Truth awakens our potential for Eternal Life (1 Cor 15:4).

Romans 8:1-14

1. THERE IS THEREFORE NOW NO CONDEMNATION TO THEM WHICH ARE IN CHRIST JESUS, WHO WALK NOT AFTER THE FLESH, BUT AFTER THE SPIRIT.

2. FOR THE LAW OF THE SPIRIT OF LIFE IN CHRIST JESUS HATH MADE ME FREE FROM THE LAW OF SIN AND DEATH.

3. FOR WHAT THE LAW COULD NOT DO, IN THAT IT WAS WEAK THROUGH THE FLESH, GOD SENDING HIS OWN SON IN THE LIKENESS OF SINFUL FLESH, AND FOR SIN, CONDEMNED SIN IN THE FLESH:

4. THAT THE RIGHTEOUSNESS OF THE LAW MIGHT BE FULFILLED IN US, WHO WALK NOT AFTER THE FLESH, BUT AFTER THE SPIRIT.

5. FOR THEY THAT ARE AFTER THE FLESH DO MIND THE THINGS OF THE FLESH; BUT THEY THAT ARE AFTER THE SPIRIT THE THINGS OF THE SPIRIT.

6. FOR TO BE CARNALLY MINDED IS DEATH; BUT TO BE SPIRITUALLY MINDED IS LIFE AND PEACE.

7. BECAUSE THE CARNAL MIND IS ENMITY AGAINST GOD: FOR IT IS NOT SUBJECT TO THE LAW OF GOD, NEITHER INDEED CAN BE.

8. SO THEN THEY THAT ARE IN THE FLESH CANNOT PLEASE GOD.

9. BUT YE ARE NOT IN THE FLESH, BUT IN THE SPIRIT, IF SO BE THAT THE SPIRIT OF GOD DWELL IN YOU. NOW IF ANY MAN HAVE NOT THE SPIRIT OF CHRIST, HE IS NONE OF HIS.

10. AND IF CHRIST BE IN YOU, THE BODY IS DEAD BECAUSE OF SIN; BUT THE SPIRIT IS LIFE BECAUSE OF RIGHTEOUSNESS.

11. BUT IF THE SPIRIT OF HIM THAT RAISED UP JESUS FROM THE DEAD DWELL IN YOU, HE THAT RAISED UP CHRIST FROM THE DEAD SHALL ALSO QUICKEN YOUR MORTAL BODIES BY HIS SPIRIT THAT DWELLETH IN YOU.

12. THEREFORE, BRETHREN, WE ARE DEBTORS, NOT TO THE FLESH, TO LIVE AFTER THE FLESH.

FOR IF YE LIVE AFTER THE FLESH, YE SHALL DIE: BUT IF YE THROUGH THE SPIRIT DO MORTIFY THE DEEDS OF THE BODY, YE SHALL LIVE.

Preparing To Translate

The Prophesies of Daniel According to Kabbalah, Chapter 8, Alternate Translation, was researched in March of 2015, and preached in two separate meetings as *Christ-Centered Kabbalah* Message #831, *A History of Adam.*

Three Hebrew-English dictionaries, three Interlinear Texts, and multiple Bible Dictionaries (see, Table of Authorities at the beginning of *this Book*) were used to search out the meaning of each Hebrew word of Daniel, Chapter 8. English dictionaries, encyclopedias and search engines, were also employed to acquire as much information as possible about obviously, and not so obviously related topics, which were revealed through the *Alternate Translations*.

Each word and verse was seriously prayed over to discover God's spiritual message behind the written words.

The Prophecies of Daniel, Chapter 8, Accorcing to Kabbalah, Alternate Translation, contains a Table of References, as well as an Appendix for each verse, which includes the Notes created for that verse as CCK Message #831, *A History of Adam*, was preached.

It is not unusual for the verse structure of the *Alternate Translations* to be rearranged so that they can be read as one continuous message. Accordingly, some paragraph numbers are out of order (*3* before *2*, for example) and some paragraphs are divided into *a* and *b* and interspersed (*2a, 3a, 2b, 3b,* for example).

Alternate Translations Are Progressive

Alternate Translations were rendered for each verse in its entirety. After that, all of the translated verses are read together as one whole revelation, to confirm their synchronicity, reveal additional, deep nuances of the whole revelation, and to expose any inconsistencies or errors.

Alternate Translations are progressive in that the *Alternate Translation* for each verse is affected by the *Alternate Translations* for previous and subsequent verses. A newly translated verse, for example, will be influenced by previous Alternate Translations, and sometimes the Alternate Translation for the new verse causes changes in previously translated verses.

The Torah (The Word of God) Is Alive

The *Alternate Translation* of one whole chapter of Scripture is a living organism that evolves and grows in scope. The Spirit of Revelation refines the *Alternate Translations* as the translator reads and re-reads them. Eventually, all of the thoughts, understanding and influences of the Carnal Mind are removed, and the optimal understanding for that particular time, is reached.

Accordingly, you will find several versions of *Daniel, Chapter 8*, in this Book, which represent the progression of the *Alternate Translation* from its beginning to its final stage:

1. The King James Version [KJV]

2. The Alternate, Amplified Translation [ATB]

3. The Alternate Amplified Translation – Annotated [ATB]

Written words are vessels that clothe the spiritual word, just like the body is a vessel that carries the soul in this world. It might even be said that the spiritual understanding of a written word is the soul of that written word.

Unveiling the spiritual meaning of a word shatters its hard exterior, so that the spiritual contents flow out and blend with the spiritual contents of the other vessels. *The Spirit of Revelation* takes hold of the Torah (Word of God) in this *liquid form,* goes beyond the letter of the Word, and reveals the esoteric message of the Torah (Word of God) for a particular people, at an appointed time.

Sheila R Vitale

King James Translation
Exodus, Chapter 32

Exodus, Chapter 32

King James Version

1 And when the people saw that Moses delayed to come down out of the mount, the people gathered themselves together unto Aaron, and said unto him, Up, make us gods, which shall go before us; for as for this Moses, the man that brought us up out of the land of Egypt, we wot not what is become of him.

2 And Aaron said unto them, Break off the golden earrings, which are in the ears of your wives, of your sons, and of your daughters, and bring them unto me.

3 And all the people brake off the golden earrings which were in their ears, and brought them unto Aaron.

4 And he received them at their hand, and fashioned it with a graving tool, after he had made it a molten calf: and they said, These be thy gods, O Israel, which brought thee up out of the land of Egypt.

5 And when Aaron saw it, he built an altar before it; and Aaron made proclamation, and said, To morrow is a feast to the Lord.

6 And they rose up early on the morrow, and offered burnt offerings, and brought peace offerings; and the people sat down to eat and to drink, and rose up to play.

7 And the LORD said unto Moses, Go, get thee down; for thy people, which thou broughtest out of the land of Egypt, have corrupted themselves:

8 They have turned aside quickly out of the way which I commanded them: they have made them a molten calf, and have worshipped it, and have sacrificed thereunto, and said, These be thy gods, O Israel, which have brought thee up out of the land of Egypt.

9 And the LORD said unto Moses, I have seen this people, and, behold, it is a stiffnecked people:

10 Now therefore let me alone, that my wrath may wax hot against them, and that I may consume them: and I will make of thee a great nation.

11 And Moses besought the LORD his God, and said, LORD , why doth thy wrath wax hot against thy people, which thou hast brought forth out of the land of Egypt with great power, and with a mighty hand?

12 Wherefore should the Egyptians speak, and say, For mischief did he bring them out, to slay them in the mountains, and to consume them from the face of the earth? Turn from thy fierce wrath, and repent of this evil against thy people.

13 Remember Abraham, Isaac, and Israel, thy servants, to whom thou swarest by thine own self, and saidst unto them, I will multiply your seed as the stars of heaven, and all this land that I have spoken of will I give unto your seed, and they shall inherit it for ever.

14 And the LORD repented of the evil which he thought to do unto his people.

15 And Moses turned, and went down from the mount, and the two tables of the testimony were in his hand: the tables were written on both their sides; on the one side and on the other were they written.

16 And the tables were the work of God, and the writing was the writing of God, graven upon the tables.

17 And when Joshua heard the noise of the people as they shouted, he said unto Moses, There is a noise of war in the camp.

18 And he said, It is not the voice of them that shout for mastery, neither is it the voice of them that cry for being overcome: but the noise of them that sing do I hear.

19 And it came to pass, as soon as he came nigh unto the camp, that he saw the calf, and the dancing: and Moses' anger waxed hot, and he cast the tables out of his hands, and brake them beneath the mount.

20 And he took the calf which they had made, and burnt it in the fire, and ground it to powder, and strawed it upon the water, and made the children of Israel drink of it.

21 And Moses said unto Aaron, What did this people unto thee, that thou hast brought so great a sin upon them?

22 And Aaron said, Let not the anger of my lord wax hot: thou knowest the people, that they are set on mischief.

23 For they said unto me, Make us gods, which shall go before us: for as for this Moses, the man that brought us up out of the land of Egypt, we wot not what is become of him.

24 And I said unto them, Whosoever hath any gold, let them break it off. So they gave it me: then I cast it into the fire, and there came out this calf.

25 And when Moses saw that the people were naked; (for Aaron had made them naked unto their shame among their enemies:)

26 Then Moses stood in the gate of the camp, and said, Who is on the LORD's side? let him come unto me. And all the sons of Levi gathered themselves together unto him.

27 And he said unto them, Thus saith the LORD God of Israel, Put every man his sword by his side, and go in and out from gate to gate throughout the camp, and slay every man his brother, and every man his companion, and every man his neighbour.

28 And the children of Levi did according to the word of Moses: and there fell of the people that day about three thousand men.

29 For Moses had said, Consecrate yourselves to day to the LORD , even every man upon his son, and upon his brother; that he may bestow upon you a blessing this day.

30 And it came to pass on the morrow, that Moses said unto the people, Ye have sinned a great sin: and now I will go up unto the LORD ; peradventure I shall make an atonement for your sin.

31 And Moses returned unto the LORD , and said, Oh, this people have sinned a great sin, and have made them gods of gold.

32 Yet now, if thou wilt forgive their sin; and if not, blot me, I pray thee, out of thy book which thou hast written.

33 And the LORD said unto Moses, Whosoever hath sinned against me, him will I blot out of my book.

34 Therefore now go, lead the people unto the place of which I have spoken unto thee: behold, mine Angel shall go before thee: nevertheless in the day when I visit I will visit their sin upon them.

35 And the LORD plagued the people, because they made the calf, which Aaron made.

KJV

Alternate, Amplified Translation
Exodus, Chapter 32

Exodus, Chapter 32

Fear Of Abandonment

1a Now, when Moses did not descend from the mountain [as quickly as] the people expected [him to, their hearts] fainted [from fear; and]

Emotional & Spiritual Weakness

1b They shamefully transferred their allegiance [from Moses] to Aaron, saying,

1c "We do not know what happened to this man, Moses, [who] empowered us to ascend above the spiritual [waters] of Egypt,

1d [So, you, Aaron, must be the one who is supposed] to stand up [in spiritual power] and make our bodies the chariots that carry Elohim,"

2a And Aaron said to [the people], "listen to me,

2b The mixed multitude, that idolatrous, male nature of the [Serpent's] Circular Universe, [has taken you to be his] wives, [and,

2c Unless the spiritual military] power of [Jehovah] rescues [Abel], the royal [female] seed of the Shekinah [within you],

2d You will be guilty of shedding the blood of [Abel all over again];" and

3a All the people listened to what Aaron [said about their being guilty of] shedding the blood of [Abel, the Shekinah's] royal [female seed], again, and

5a The widowed personalities of [the people repented, and Righteous Adam,

A New Nature

4a Aaron's] splendid [spiritual] covering, interacted intimately with [Abel within the people, who] had said,

4b "These [two men, Moses and Aaron, are] your Gods, O Israel, which brought you up above the spiritual waters of the land of Egypt," and

6a [The people] drank [the Water of Life] from [the well of the Shekinah within Aaron], and

6b Ate [the manna that congeals into the female Adam], who produces the lamb, which represents the neck [energy center of Righteous Adam, and

4c Righteous Adam within Aaron], seized the [male calf] mind of [the mixed multitude within the people, and]

4d Engraved [Abel, the spiritual side of the male calf] mind, [with the nature of Jehovah], and

4e Shaped [Cain], the [animal side of the male calf] mind [of the people which were engraved with the nature of Jehovah, into the female Adam], and

Spiritual Sacrifices

5b When Aaron saw that Righteous Adam, the [spiritual] altar [upon which the male calf mind of the mixed multitude] is [sacrificed, was re]built [within the people],

5c Aaron called for [the people] to bring forth [the male calf mind of the mixed multitude from within themselves, so that

5d The Shekinah's fiery stream within Aaron] could crush [the male calf mind which was formed as a result of Abel's adultery with the female power], and

5e Bring the next day [of creation into existence within them], and

6c The people offered up [their male calf mind, the fruit of Abel's adultery with the female power], as a peace offering [to Jehovah], and

3b That is how [Righteous Adam], the spiritual, [military] power [of Jehovah within] Aaron, rescued [Abel, the royal female seed of the Shekinah within the people, from] the idolatrous [calf nature of the mixed multitude of the Serpent's] Circular Universe, [and after that],

5f The third day [of creation came into existence within the people, and

Aaron Mocked

6d Jehovah] married the people [again, but]

6e [Cain, the animal side of the male calf mind of the mixed multitude] rose up to mock [Aaron]

8a Very soon [after Aaron rescued the people, and Cain, the animal side of]

8b The male calf [mind of the mixed multitude],

8c Sacrificed [Abel, the royal female seed of the Shekinah, to Satan, the female power], and

8d [Satan], the female [power]

8e Interacted intimately with [Abel, who was under Cain's influence, and

8f Abel] submitted to

8g [Cain, and to Satan, the female power], and that is how [Cain, the animal side of the mixed multitude],

8h Covered [over Abel, who is engraved with Jehovah's righteous nature, and

8i Turned [the people] away from the lifestyle [that Moses] commanded them [to follow], and

8j The people spoke the blasphemous words [of the mixed multitude], saying,

8k "[The male calf, mind of] these [Israelites, the fruit of the union of Abel and Satan, the female power], are your gods, O Israel, which empowered you to ascend above the spiritual [waters] of the material land of Egypt," and

Pharaoh's Neck

9a Jehovah said to Moses, "I have looked into [the heart of] this people

7a Which ascended above the [spiritual] waters of [the material land of] Egypt, and

9b I see that

7b [Satan, the female power] has married [my nature that you, Moses, formed in] them, and

9c [Completed them, and that the people are expressing] the cruelty of [Pharaoh's] neck [energy center]," and

Completed Personalities

7c Jehovah said to Moses, "go down to [the Circular world of the Universe of Separation], and

10a Burn the male [calf mind that] the Serpent [formed within the people], and

10b Complete [Cain, the personality of] the ox that is nailed to the [lower] window of [creation, and]

10c Complete [the physical bodies of] the ox [of Israel], that great, widowed nation that is nailed to the [lower] window [of creation, so that

10d They may remain [in the earth];" and

Blind To Sin

11a Jehovah, the God [of Israel], said to Moses,

11b "The personalities of my people [who] you are married to, are spiritually sick [concerning their inability to recognize their sins], and

12e They have become] Egyptians [again], so

11c [Satan, the expression of my] anger [and the enforcer of my righteous Sowing & Reaping Judgment], is raging against the [idolatrous, male calf] mind [of the mixed multitude within] my people, who

11d Elohim, the great strength of my authority [in the earth, just] raised up above [the spiritual] waters of the material Land of Egypt, [and]

12a [Their false] gods are speaking to them [saying that you,

12b Moses], had an evil motive for bringing them out of captivity, [and that

12c You intend] to slay them, [and]

12d Consume their [spiritual] energy, [which is] greater than the energy of their earthen bodies,

Jehovah's Promise

13a [But], I have remembered [my promises to] Abraham, Isaac and Israel, my servants, to whom I swore by my own self, saying,

13b '[The female Adam, Abraham's] seed, shall increase into [many]

13c Permanently fixed points of [spiritual] light in the heaven [of the Universe of Beriah], and

13d They shall be [the inner dimension of the immortal], earthen [bodies] that I told [Jacob] about, [who] I gave the [royal female] seed [of the Shekinah to], and

13e [Israel] shall possess eternal life;' and

Reprieve

12b [That is the reason why] I am granting the repentance [to my people, that] comes from an higher [authority than that of Satan], the rage of my anger, [so that]

12c The evil [that Satan, the enforcer of the Sowing & Reaping Judgment, is devising] against my widowed people, shall be turned back;" and

14 Jehovah, breathed strongly against [Satan, the one who executes] the evil that [Jehovah] said he would do to his widowed people; and

A Spiritual Mind

15a Moses turned [toward the material world below], and

15b Went down [from the mountain of God] with two [additional spiritual grades], and

15c One [of the two is] the spiritual region [in Moses'] heart [center which is] across from the [spiritual] waters [of the material land of Egypt], and

15d The [other] one of the two [is] the spiritual mind [that resides there, which is] engraved with the spiritual [authority of] the male [Adam],

15e The [true and faithful] witness [that]

Engraved By God

16a The work of God

15f Is written

16b In the framework [of a man's heart], and [that]

16c They [who] write the writings of God [in the vernacular] are, themselves, engraved [with the nature of] the framer in the upper window [of creation]; and

Sin Recognized

17a Joshua, [Moses' spiritual] mate, heard the loud shouts of the people [and] said to Moses,

17b "[This] noise [is] the noise of the warlike military power [that opposes God, not the sound of people worshiping God," and]

The Second Witness

18a The Eternal One spoke [through Moses, who is spiritually] male [to Joshua], saying,

18b "[It is true], I hear the voice [of Abel, who] Cain defeated,

18c Crying out [for the spiritual food that forms Adam's male [mind] within the people, even

18d While they] are obeying the voice of [Satan], the female power," and

Inclined To Do Evil

21 Moses said to Aaron, "what sin did the people do that brought this great [judgment] upon them?" and

22a Aaron said, "lord, [Moses], do not let your anger rise up, [because the people] are saying,

23a 'We do not know what happened to this man, Moses, [who] empowered us to ascend above the spiritual [waters] of Egypt, [so,

23b You, Aaron, must be the one who is supposed] to stand up [in spiritual power] and make our bodies the chariots that carry Elohim,' [because]

22b You know that the people are inclined to do evil, and

24a I [have already] told them [that] they must throw down the gold[en calf that they made, and that]

24b They will have to give up [the male calf mind] that [Satan, the female power], formed in them, [before they can] be circumcised in the Shekinah's fiery stream, [which

24c Frees Abel, the Shekinah's royal female seed within them], and reforms him [into the male Adam again];" and

Bound To Pharaoh

30a It came to pass [that] the [next] day, after [Aaron spoke to Moses, that],

Widowhood

25b Moses saw that [Pharaoh], the enemy [of the Shekinah], had risen up [in spiritual power within the people]

25c [Who were Aaron's spiritual mate, and made] Aaron a widow, and a laughingstock, [and that]

25a The people were naked [because] they were no longer bound [to Jehovah], and

A Great Sin

30b Moses said to the people, "you have sinned a great sin, so

30c I will ascend before Jehovah [to see if], perhaps, [He will permit you] to atone for the sin of [the male calf mind that the female power formed in you]," and

Power For Themselves

31a Moses returned to Jehovah, and said, "Alas, the people have sinned a great sin:

31b [These] Elohim have spun the [spiritual] gold [of the Shekinah into a source of spiritual power for] themselves;" and

33a Jehovah said, "[the people] have sinned against the Shekinah, and [according to my righteous Law],

33b They should be blotted out of my Book [of Life]," and

Moses Intercedes

32a Moses [said], "please [give me] time [to teach the people how to not sin against you, so that]

32b You might forgive them [for making a golden calf], and

32c Blot out [the judgment for] the sin [of idolatry that] is written against them] in your spiritual book," and

34a Jehovah said, "Go now, then, and lead the people that belong to you [in the right path], so that

34b On the day that I told you [about,

34c When] I visit [Israel] from above, to search out [the sins that the people hide behind their] personalities,

34d [The male Adam], the angel [of the covenant that I made with Istael], shall have gone [forth to cover their inclination to do evil]," and

Sowing & Reaping

35a Jehovah plagued the people because

35b They married [Satan], the female power [that] made [them strong enough to influence] Aaron to make

35c A [golden] calf [for them], and

26a Moses stood up in the doorway [between the mortal and the immortal worlds], where [Satan, the female] military power [that married Abel had entered into the people], and said,

Priests Challenged

26b "The Shekinah and Jehovah are with me, all you sons of Levi, [so]

26c Depart from your [spiritual] adultery [with Pharaoh, before Jehovah's Sowing & Reaping Judgment falls upon you], " and [then]

Mortal Men Challenged

27a Moses said to the mortal men [who were adulterously attached to Pharaoh],

27b "Thus says Jehovah, the God of Israel,

27c 'I am bringing [Righteous Adam, my] military power [from [the immortal side of] the doorway, into the [spiritual universe that your male calf] mind [rolled out on the mortal side of] the doorway, [and]

27d His drawn sword is going to slay [the male calf mind that the female power made from Abel], your [spiritual] generative part, [and

27e [He is going to sever] Cain, [Abel's] brother, [the conscious part of] the Evil Inclination which is in every mortal man, [from Leviathan], the companion [of Satan, the unconscious part of the Evil Inclination] which is in every mortal man," and

28b The mortal men [called upon Pharaoh to save them, but he did not answer], and

Seized & Slain

28a The wisdom of [Pharaoh], the third [degree of] the unholy spiritual power [within] the children of Levi who [abandoned their adulterous relationship with Pharaoh], as Moses told them to, fell down that day, [because]

The Female Power Burned

19a It came to pass [that], as Moses approached [the people who are Jehovah's] armies, and

19b Saw the spiritual activity of the [male] calf [mind that Satan, the Serpent's female] military power, [had formed within the people who were Moses'] mate, Elohim,

20a [The Spirit within Righteous Adam, the male] mind [of Moses, Jehovah's] mate, seized the [male] calf [mind that Satan, the female power], had made, and

20b The fiery stream [of the Shekinah within Moses], burnt [the male calf mind that Cain, the animal side of the mixed multitude, had sacrificed Abe to make, and

20c The Shekinah's fiery stream] crushed [the male calf mind, and

20d The five male sefirot of the female Adam] separated from [Pharaoh, and

Seed & Water

20e Moses] spread the [royal female] seed of [the Shekinah] upon the [earthen] personalities of [the Levite priests of] Israel, His mate, and

20f Gave [their earthen] bodies, [the Water of Life] to drink, [and]

Jehovah Is God

29a Moses, the son of Righteous Adam, told [the people of Israel, his] widowed wife,

29b [That Jehovah] would, indeed, bless the mortal men of [Israel with a spiritual male child, which would make them] the relatives [of God], and that,

29c In that day, [the Shekinah] would, fill [the people of Israel] with Living Water, and [that]

29d [Righteous Adam], would give [the people of Israel] the [female reproductive] seed [of the Shekinah from the world] above, [which is the foundation out of which Jehovah's] male mind [springs].

The 1ˢᵗ Sin
Idolatry For Leaders

Idolatry

Idolatry[1] is dependency upon something, or someone, other than God. Interests that interfere with prayer and study time, or admiration of persons whose opinions we hold more dear than the Word of God, are all examples of idolatry in our everyday lives. Idolatry for teachers is another ever-present danger, but God helps true seekers to distinguish between respect and idolatry.

Fear Of Abandonment

1a Now, when Moses did not descend from the mountain [as quickly as] the people expected [him to, their hearts] fainted [from fear; and]

---

[1] **Idolatry**

Ex 20:3 – No other Gods

> ³Thou shalt have no other gods before me.
>
> KJV

Emotional & Spiritual Weakness[2]

1b They shamefully transferred their allegiance [from Moses] to Aaron, saying,

1c "We do not know what happened to this man, Moses, [who] empowered us to ascend above the spiritual [waters][3] of Egypt,

1d [So, you, Aaron, must be the one who is supposed] to stand up[4] [in spiritual power][(Note 74)] and make our bodies[(Note 41)] the chariots that carry Elohim," [5]

---

[2] **Emotional And Spiritual Weakness**

Aaron taught the people that it is possible to **unwittingly** idolize their leaders and make them objects of worship, which . . . . (Read Whole Footnote in Footnote Appendix)

[3] **Spiritual Waters**

The spiritual waters of Egypt are the Egyptian Astral Plane (unholy Yetzirah) . . . . (Read Whole Footnote in Footnote Appendix)

[4] **Stand up in God's power**

To stand up suggests the spiritual strength and authority of manhood.

[5] **A Cart For Elohim**

The animal nature generates and is in control of the body, but in the days of Messiah,* Righteous Adam, the soul of . . . . (Read Whole Footnote in Footnote Appendix)

Aaron Judges

The 1st Sin

Deliverance From Fear Of Abandonment

Abel's Blood Guilt

Aaron had the spiritual authority of the female
Shekinah, to forgive sins through understanding.
Aaron did NOT have the male spiritual authority to punish sin.
Aaron was a teacher who convinced the people that
fear had opened them to seduction by an unclean power, and
The people offered up their Animal Nature to Jehovah, voluntarily.
The Shekinah within Aaron
burnt the unholy calf mind within the people,
with their permission, and the Mind of God was restored. To them

The people were delivered through
understanding and a change of mind.

Ref: The Authority of the Shekinah:
See, Aaron's splendid covering – Verse 4a, p 7

2a And Aaron said to [the people], "listen to me,

2b The mixed multitude,⁶ that idolatrous, male nature⁽Note 6⁾ of the [Serpent's] Circular Universe,⁷ [has taken you to be his] wives,⁸ [and,

2c Unless the spiritual military] power⁹ of [Jehovah] rescues [Abel], the royal [female] seed¹⁰ of the Shekinah¹¹ [within you],

---

⁶ **Mixed Multitude**

Cain and Abel are one corrupt mind called ***the mixed multitude*** .... (Read Whole Footnote in Footnote Appendix)

⁷ **Circular Universe**

The universe that we live in and are familiar with is circular, but there is also a linear universe, called ***the Image*** .... (Read Whole Footnote in Footnote Appendix)

⁸ **Spiritual Wives**

A personality can be bonded, or married to God, or to a spirit, either directly, or indirectly through another man. .... (Read Whole Footnote in Footnote Appendix)

⁹ **The Military Power of Jehovah**

Jehovah's warfare is in the spiritual plane. .... (Read Whole Footnote in Footnote Appendix)

¹⁰ **Royal Female Seed**

Abel is the Shekinah in captivity, the female seed that matures into the male calf and joins the Earth to the Heavenly .... (Read Whole Footnote in Footnote Appendix)

¹¹ **The Shekinah**

There is a Shekinah above and a Shekinah below .... (Read Whole Footnote in Footnote Appendix)

2d   You will be guilty of shedding the blood of [Abel[Notes 6, 52] all over again];" and

3a   All the people listened to what Aaron [said about their being guilty of] shedding the blood of [Abel,[Notes 6, 52] the Shekinah's] royal [female seed],[Note 10] again, and

5a   The widowed personalities[12] of [the people repented, and Righteous Adam, [13]

A New Nature

4a   Aaron's] splendid [spiritual] covering, interacted intimately[Note 12] with [Abel[Note 10] within the people, who] had said,

4b   "These [two men, Moses and Aaron, are] your Gods,[Note 1] O Israel, which brought you up above the spiritual waters[Note 3] of the land of Egypt," and

---

[12] **Spiritual Marriage**

An intimacy, or spiritual marriage, can exist between two men, and between a teacher and his disciples. .... (Read Whole Footnote in Footnote Appendix)

[13] **Righteous Adam**

Righteous Adam is the male Adam. .... (Read whole footnote in Footnote Appendix)

6a [The people] drank [the Water of Life](Notes 14, 82) from [the well[14] of the Shekinah(Note 11) within Aaron], and

6b Ate [the manna[15] that congeals[16] into the female Adam],(Note 11) who produces the lamb, which represents the neck[17] [energy center of Righteous Adam],(Note 13) and

4c [Righteous Adam(Note 13) within Aaron], seized the [male calf] mind(Note 6) of [the mixed multitude(Note 6) within the people, and]

---

[14] **Well of Existence**

The Shekinah is called a Well because she is spiritually equipped to receive, contain and propagate the ***Water of Life***. . . . (Read Whole Footnote in Footnote Appendix)

[15] **Manna Is Spiritual Food**

Manna is spiritual food. God's people in the wilderness missed the physical and emotional comforts of Egypt . . . (Read Whole Footnote in Footnote Appendix)

[16] **Manna, The Flesh Of The Shekinah**

Manna is the spiritual food that restores the broken relationship between Abel, the Shekinah in captivity . . . .(Read Whole Footnote in Footnote Appendix)

[17] **The Neck Of Righteous Adam**

The neck of Righteous Adam is called ***the Lamb***. . . .(Read Whole Footnote in Footnote Appendix)

4d   Engraved[18] [Abel, the spiritual side of the male calf] mind,(Note 6) [with the nature of Jehovah],(Note 13) and

4e   Shaped[19] [Cain, the animal side of the male calf] mind(Note 6) [of the people which were engraved(Note 14) with the nature of Jehovah,(Note 13) into the female Adam],[20] (Note 11) and

Spiritual Sacrifices

5b   When Aaron saw that Righteous Adam,(Note 13) the [spiritual] altar[21] [upon which the male calf mind(Note 61) of the

---

[18] **Engraving Tool**

The nature, or character, of a person reveals the source of their spirit . . . . (Read Whole Footnote in Footnote Appendix)

[19] **Formed From The Dust**

Jehovah's breath engraves his nature on the soul of man. . . . (Read Whole Footnote in Footnote Appendix)

[20] **The End Of The Transgression**

The soul of fallen mankind is a chameleon. It changes from righteous to evil and from evil to righteous; depending . . . . (Read Whole Footnote in Footnote Appendix)

[21] **Spiritual Altar**

The female Adam (Christ Jesus in the New Testament) is the spiritual altar of God, the place where the unholy male calf . . . . (Read Whole Footnote in Footnote Appendix)

mixed multitude](Note 6) is [sacrificed, was re]built [within the people],

5c   Aaron called for [the people] to bring forth [the male calf mind²² (Note 61) of the mixed multitude(Note 6) from within themselves, so that

5d   The Shekinah's fiery stream within Aaron] could crush(Note 79) [the male calf mind which was formed as a result of Abel's adultery(Notes 38, 61) with the female power,²³] and

5e   Bring the next day [of creation(Note 24) into existence within them], and

6c   The people offered up [their male calf(Note 61) mind, the fruit of Abel's adultery with the female power],(Note 38) as a peace offering [to Jehovah], and

3b   That is how [Righteous Adam], the spiritual, [military] power [of Jehovah(Note 9) within] Aaron, rescued [Abel, the royal female seed(Note 10) of the Shekinah(Note 11) within the people, from] the idolatrous [calf nature(Note 22) of the mixed multitude(Note 6) of the Serpent's] Circular Universe,(Note 7) [and, after that],

---

²²   **Male Calf**

  The Shekinah (note 11), and ***The Female Calf***, introduce the following subject matter. . . . . (Read Whole Footnote in Footnote Appendix)

²³   **The Female Power**

  God is in full control of all of the events in the earth . . . . (Read Whole Footnote in Footnote Appendix)

5f　　The third day [of creation[24] came into existence within the people], and

---

[24]　**Grass**

　　Grass is a symbol for the female Adam,[(Note 11)] who appeared on the third day of creation . . . .(Read Whole Footnote in Footnote Appendix)

Exodus 32:7-10

⁶And they rose up early on the morrow, and offered burnt offerings, and brought peace offerings; and the people sat down to eat and to drink, and rose up to play.

⁷And the Lord said unto Moses, Go, get thee down; for thy people, which thou broughtest out of the land of Egypt, have corrupted themselves:

⁸They have turned aside quickly out of the way which I commanded them: they have made them a molten calf, and have worshipped it, and have sacrificed thereunto, and said, These be thy gods, O Israel, which have brought thee up out of the land of Egypt.

⁹And the Lord said unto Moses, I have seen this people, and, behold, it is a stiffnecked people:

¹⁰Now therefore let me alone, that my wrath may wax hot against them, and that I may consume them: and I will make of thee a great nation.

KJV

The 2nd Sin

Self-Appointed Authority

Aaron Mocked

6d [Jehovah] married the people [again,[25] but]

6e [Cain, the animal side of the male calf mind of the mixed multitude], rose up[26] to mock[27] [Aaron]

8a Very soon [after Aaron rescued[Vs 4a] the people, and Cain, the animal side of],

8b The male calf [mind of the mixed multitude],[Note 6]

---

[25] **Bonded To Jehovah**

The people who were married to Jehovah through their *spiritual marriage* [Note 12] to Moses, lost both of their spiritual ... . (Read Whole Footnote in Footnote Appendix)

[26] **Spiritual Arrogance**

The second time the people sinned, they were no longer naïve and ignorant. .... (Read Whole Footnote in Footnote Appendix)

[27] **Cuckold**

A cuckold is an object of scorn because a man's wife took a lover. The suggestion is that the man could not satisfy her. .... (Read Whole Footnote in Footnote Appendix)

8c   Sacrificed[28] [Abel, the royal female seed of the Shekinah, to Satan, the female power],[Notes 23, 61] and

8d   [Satan], the female [power][Note 23]

8e   Interacted intimately[Notes 12, 60] with [Abel, who was under Cain's influence],[Note 53] and

8f   [Abel] submitted to

8g   [Cain, and to Satan, the female power],[Note 23] and that is how[Cain, the animal side of the mixed multitude,

8h   Covered[29] [over Abel,[Note 10] who is engraved with Jehovah's righteous nature, and][Note 13]

8i   Turned [the people] away from the lifestyle [that Moses] commanded them [to follow,[Note 25] and

---

[28]   **Idolatrous sacrifice**

The holy male calf is the only sacrifice acceptable to a pagan god. .... (Read Whole Footnote in Footnote Appendix)

[29]   **Covering**

The Hebrew word translated **molten, Strong's #4541**, is spelled with the same Hebrew letters (in the same sequence) as the following word in the Hebrew Lexicon, **Strong's 4540**. .... (Read Whole Footnote in Footnote Appendix)

8j   The people spoke the blasphemous words[30] [of the mixed multitude], saying,

8k   "[The male calf, mind of] these [Israelites, the fruit of the union of Abel and Satan, the female power], [Note 6] are your gods,[31] [Note 30] O Israel, which empowered you to ascend above the spiritual [waters][Note 3] of the material land of Egypt," and

---

[30]   **Blasphemous Words**

   Words reveal the nature and mind of the person speaking them .... (Read Whole Footnote in Footnote Appendix)

[31]   **False Gods**

   "The male and female principalities that ride on the male calf[Note 22] of the mixed multitude[Note 6] are your gods." .... (Read Whole Footnote in Footnote Appendix)

The 3rd Sin
Illegal Acquisition Of Spiritual Power

Pharaoh's Neck

9a   Jehovah said to Moses, "I have looked into [the heart of] this people[32]

7a   Which ascended above the [spiritual] waters[Note 3] of [the material land of] Egypt, and

9b   I see that

7b   [Satan, the female power], has married[Notes 18, 30] [my nature that you, Moses, formed in] them, and

9c   [Completed them, and that the people are expressing] the cruelty[33] of [Pharaoh's[Note 72]] neck [energy center], and

---

[32]   **The Wickedness Of Man**

Humanity are the descendants of the female Adam who committed adultery with the Serpent. . . . . (Read Whole Footnote in Footnote Appendix)

[33]   **Cruelty In Israel**

Israel is a chameleon. . . . . (Read Whole Footnote in Footnote Appendix 169)

Completed Personalities

7c   Jehovah said to Moses, "go down to [he Circular^(Note 7) world of the Universe of Separation], and

10a   Burn the male [calf mind that] the Serpent [formed within the people], and

10b   Complete^(Note 25) [Cain, the personality[34] of] the ox[35] that is nailed to the [lower] window of [creation, and]

10c   Complete [the physical bodies^(Note 41) of] the ox,^(Note 35) [the animal side of Israel], that great, widowed^(Note 12 25) nation that is nailed to the [lower] window [of creation, so that

10d   They may remain [in the earth];"[36] and

---

[34]   **Personality**

The emotional and intellectual aspects of the body. . . . . (Read Whole Footnote in Footnote Appendix)

[35]   **Ox**

The body, including its emotional and intellectual aspects. . . . . (Read Whole Footnote in Footnote Appendix171)

[36]   **Immortality**

All Israel shall attain immortality in the world to come. . . . . (Read Whole Footnote in Footnote Appendix)

Exodus 32:11-14

¹¹And Moses besought the Lord his God, and said, Lord, why doth thy wrath wax hot against thy people, which thou hast brought forth out of the land of Egypt with great power, and with a mighty hand?

¹²Wherefore should the Egyptians speak, and say, For mischief did he bring them out, to slay them in the mountains, and to consume them from the face of the earth? Turn from thy fierce wrath, and repent of this evil against thy people.

¹³Remember Abraham, Isaac, and Israel, thy servants, to whom thou swarest by thine own self, and saidst unto them, I will multiply your seed as the stars of heaven, and all this land that I have spoken of will I give unto your seed, and they shall inherit it forever.

¹⁴And the Lord repented of the evil which he thought to do unto his people.

KJV

Blind To Sin

11a Jehovah, the God [of Israel], said to Moses,

11b "The personalities^(Note 34) of my people [who] you are married to,^(Note 25) are spiritually sick [concerning their inability to recognize their sins],^(Note 31a) and

12e They have become] Egyptians [again], so

11c [Satan, the expression of my] anger^(Notes 42, 44) [and the enforcer³⁷ of my righteous Sowing & Reaping Judgment],^(Note 42) is raging^(Note 37) against the [idolatrous, male calf] mind [of the mixed multitude^(Note 6) within] my people, who

11d Elohim, the great strength of my authority^(Note 48) [in the earth, just] raised up above [the spiritual] waters^(Note 3) of the material Land of Egypt, [and]

12a [Their false] gods³⁸ are speaking to them [saying that you,

---

³⁷ **The Enforcer**

Satan is the enforcer of Jehovah's righteous Sowing & Reaping Judgment..... (Read Whole Footnote in Footnote Appendix173)

³⁸ **Idolatrous Communication**

Communication such as **speaking to**, or **hearing from**, spiritual entities, is the worship of false gods, which is idolatry.... . (Read Whole Footnote, in Footnote Appendix174)

12b [Moses], had an evil motive for bringing them out of captivity,(Notes 8, 79) [and that

12c You intend] to slay them, [and]

12d Consume their [spiritual] energy, [which is] greater than the energy of their earthen bodies;

An Immortal Body

Heb 10:5 KJV

5 Wherefore when he cometh into the world, he saith,
Sacrifice and offering thou wouldest not,
but a body hast thou prepared me:

Jehovah's Promise

13a   [But], I have remembered [my promises to] Abraham, Isaac and Israel, my servants, to whom I swore by my own self, saying,

13b   '[The female Adam, Abraham's] seed,[39] shall increase into [many]

13c   Permanently fixed points of [spiritual] light in the heaven [of the Universe of Asiyah], and

13d   They shall be [the inner dimension of the immortal], earthen [bodies[40]] that I told [Jacob] about, [who] I gave the [royal female] seed [Note 10] [of the Shekinah[Note 11] to], and

13e   [Israel] shall possess eternal life;' [41] [Notes 36, 40] and

---

[39]   **Abraham's Seed**

Abraham's seed is righteous Adam in the earth of humanity. . . . . (Read Whole Footnote in Footnote Appendix)

[40]   **A Physical Body**

Righteous Adam, Jehovah's Son, shall join with Abraham's seed, the female Adam in the earth of humanity, and she shall give birth to a Son: . . . . . (Read Whole Footnote in Footnote Appendix)

[41]   **A Spiritual Body**

Adam's soul shall be given a different, incorruptible form . . . . (Read Whole Footnote in Footnote Appendix)

Reprieve

12b [That is the reason why] I am granting repentance [to my people, that] comes from an higher [authority than that of Satan], the rage of my anger,[42] [so that]

12c The evil [that Satan,[Note 37] the enforcer of the Sowing & Reaping Judgment, is devising] against my widowed[Note 12] people, shall be turned back";[43] and

---

[42] **Sowing & Reaping**

The Sowing & Reaping Judgment is the expression of Jehovah's Anger .... (Read Whole Footnote in Footnote Appendix)

[43] **Satan Turned Back**

Jehovah's mercy opposes his own righteous Sowing & Reaping Judgment..... (Read Whole Footnote in Footnote Appendix)

14 Jehovah, breathed strongly against [Satan,(Note 37) the one who executes] the evil⁴⁴ (Note 42) that [Jehovah] said he would do to his widowed people;(Note 12) and

---

⁴⁴ **Good Or Evil**

Jehovah gives us a choice: . . . . (Read Whole Footnote in Footnote Appendix)

Exodus 32:15-18

¹⁵*And Moses turned, and went down from the mount, and the two tables of the testimony were in his hand: the tables were written on both their sides; on the one side and on the other were they written.*

¹⁶*And the tables were the work of God, and the writing was the writing of God, graven upon the tables.*

¹⁷*And when Joshua heard the noise of the people as they shouted, he said unto Moses, There is a noise of war in the camp.*

¹⁸*And he said, It is not the voice of them that shout for mastery, neither is it the voice of them that cry for being overcome: but the noise of them that sing do I hear.*

KJV

A Spiritual Mind

15a Moses turned [toward the material world below],(Note 7) and

15b Went down [from the mountain of God] with two[45] [additional spiritual grades], and

15c One [of the two is] the spiritual region[46] [in Moses'] heart [center which is] across from the [spiritual] waters [of the material land of Egypt], and

---

[45] **Heart Center**

Jehovah gave Moses two additional spiritual regions from the world to come..... (Read Whole Footnote in Footnote Appendix)

[46] **Another Country**

A Neshamah that is permanently joined to a body, **rolls out** a material environment for itself, which manifests itself as .... (Read Whole Footnote in Footnote Appendix)

15d The [other] one of the two [is] the spiritual mind[47] [that resides there, which is] engraved[(Note 18)] with the spiritual [authority[48] of] the male [Adam],[(Note 82)]

15e The [true and faithful] witness[49] [that]

Engraved By God

16a The work of God,[50]

15f Is written

16b In the framework [of a man's heart], and [that]

---

[47] **Neshamah**

There are five grades of soul: . . . . (Read Whole Footnote in Footnote Appendix)

[48] **The Will Of God**

The Will of God manifested as the spiritual, government of Righteous Adam,[(Note 13)] **dries up** the waters of Satan's . . . . (Read Whole Footnote in Footnote Appendix)

[49] **Witnesses**

The Neshamah is the male mind of God. . . . . (Read Whole Footnote in Footnote Appendix)

[50] **Elohim, The Judge**

Elohim literally means **God,** or **judge** . . . . (Read Whole Footnote in Footnote Appendix)

16c They [who] write the writings of God [in the vernacular] are, themselves, engraved^(Note 18) [with the nature^(Note 13) of] the framer in the upper window [of creation]; and

Moses Judges

The 2nd Sin

Deliverance from Fear Of Authority

The People's Fear Of Losing Moses
Turns Into Rejection And
Outright Defiance Of
All That He Taught Them

Moses had the Authority to destroy their unholy calf mind
and form an authoritative soul tie, without their
permission: Verse 10, p 49

Sin Recognized

17a Joshua, [Moses' spiritual] mate,[51] (Note 12) heard the loud shouts of the people [and] said to Moses,

17b [This] noise [is] the noise of the warlike military power(Note 27) [that opposes God, not the sound of people worshiping God, and]

The Second Witness

18a The Eternal One spoke [through Moses, who is spiritually] male [to Joshua],(Notes 12, 51) saying,

18b "[It is true], I hear the voice [of Abel,(Note 10) who] Cain defeated,[52]

---

[51] **Moses & Joshua**

Joshua, the Ephraimite, and Moses, had a teacher-disciple intimacy, and Miriam and Aaron were jealous. . . . . (Read Whole Footnote in Footnote Appendix)

[52] **Abel Lives**

Joshua in verse 17, and the Eternal One speaking through Moses in verse 18, are the two witnesses required by law . . . . (Read Whole Footnote in Footnote Appendix)

18c Crying out^(Note 52) [for the spiritual food that forms Adam's male [mind] within the people, even

18d While they] are obeying⁵³ the voice of [Satan], the female power,^(Note 23) and

---

⁵³ **Cain's Control**

Cain is a serpent like his father. . . . . (Read Whole Footnote in Footnote Appendix)

Exodus 32:21-25

²¹*And Moses said unto Aaron, What did this people unto thee, that thou hast brought so great a sin upon them?*

²²*And Aaron said, Let not the anger of my lord wax hot: thou knowest the people, that they are set on mischief.*

²³*For they said unto me, Make us gods, which shall go before us: for as for this Moses, the man that brought us up out of the land of Egypt, we wot not what is become of him.*

²⁴*And I said unto them, Whosoever hath any gold, let them break it off. So they gave it me: then I cast it into the fire, and there came out this calf.*

²⁵*And when Moses saw that the people were naked; (for Aaron had made them naked unto their shame among their enemies:)*

KJV

Inclined To Do Evil

21   Moses said to Aaron, "what sin did the people do that brought this great [judgment] upon them?" and

22a   Aaron said, "lord, [Moses], do not let your anger[54] rise up [because the people] are saying,

23a   'We do not know what happened to this man, Moses, [who] empowered us to ascend above the spiritual [waters][(Note 3)] of Egypt, [so,

23b   You, Aaron, must be the one who is supposed] to stand up[(Note 4)] [in spiritual power] and make our bodies[(Note 41)] the chariots[(Note 5)] that carry Elohim,' [(Note 50)] [because]

22b   You know that the people are inclined to do evil,[55] and

24a   I [have already] told them that they must throw down the gold[en calf that they made, and that]

24b   They will have to give up [the male calf mind][(Notes 61)] that [Satan, the female power], formed in them, [before they

---

[54]   **Lord *and* Master**

Adon is a masculine noun which means **lord** or **master**. The most frequent use of the word is a ***human lord***, but it is also used of divinity. . . . . (Read Whole Footnote in Footnote Appendix)

[55]   **Evil Sons**

Aaron and Moses knew that the people had ***an evil inclination.*** . . . . (Read Whole Footnote in Footnote Appendix)

can] be circumcised[56] in the Shekinah's fiery stream, (Note 78) [which

24c Frees Abel, (Notes 61,) the Shekinah's royal female seed within them], and reforms him [into the male Adam again];" and

---

[56] **Spiritual Circumcision**

Circumcise yourself!

Cut off Cain, the foreskin of the unholy male calf that joins you to the female power. . . . . (Read Whole Footnote in Footnote Appendix)

Moses Judges The 3rd Sin

Deliverance From Fear of Pharaoh
(See, Note 72)

Bound To Pharaoh

30a It came to pass [that] the [next] day, after [Aaron spoke to Moses, that]

Widowhood

25b Moses saw that [Pharaoh],^(Note 23) the enemy [of the Shekinah],^(Note 11) had risen up[57] [in spiritual power within the people]

25c [Who were Aaron's spiritual mate, and made Aaron] a widow,^(Note 12) and a laughingstock,^(Note 27) [and that]

---

[57] **Idolatry & The Serpent**

Idolatry in Israel strengthens the Serpent. . . . . (Read Whole Footnote in Footnote Appendix)

25a   The people were naked,[58] [because] they were no longer bound [to Jehovah[59]], and

---

[58]   **Naked**

The people were loosed from Jehovah, their spiritual cover.... . (Read Whole Footnote in Footnote Appendix)

[59]   **Separated From God**

The Torah (Word of God) ***is symbolized by water.*** .... (Read Whole Footnote in Footnote Appendix)

Exodus 32:30-35

³⁰And it came to pass on the morrow, that Moses said unto the people, Ye have sinned a great sin: and now I will go up unto the Lord; peradventure I shall make an atonement for your sin.

³¹And Moses returned unto the Lord, and said, Oh, this people have sinned a great sin, and have made them gods of gold.

³²Yet now, if thou wilt forgive their sin; and if not, blot me, I pray thee, out of thy book which thou hast written.

³³And the Lord said unto Moses, Whosoever hath sinned against me, him will I blot out of my book.

³⁴Therefore now go, lead the people unto the place of which I have spoken unto thee: behold, mine Angel shall go before thee: nevertheless in the day when I visit I will visit their sin upon them.

³⁵And the Lord plagued the people, because they made the calf, which Aaron made.

KJV

A Great Sin

30b   Moses said to the people, "you have sinned a great sin,(Note 61) so

30c   I will ascend before Jehovah [to see if], perhaps, [He will permit you] to atone(Note 61) for the sin of [the male calf, that the female power(Note 23) formed in you]," and

Power For Themselves

31a   Moses returned to Jehovah, and said, "Alas, the people have sinned a great sin:

31b   [These] Elohim[60] have spun the [spiritual] gold [of the Shekinah(Note 11) into a source of spiritual power(Note 74) for] themselves;"(Note 74) and

---

[60]   **Ye Are Gods**

Eternal life is a potential reality for human beings who are imbued with a soul that comes from God. . . . . (Read Whole Footnote in Footnote Appendix)

33a Jehovah said, "[the people] have sinned against the Shekinah,[61] (Notes 74,) and [according to my righteous Law],

33b They should be blotted out[62] of my Book [of Life],"[63] and

Moses Intercedes

32a Moses [said], "please [give me] time [to teach the people how to not sin against you, so that]

---

[61] **Unholy Male Calf**

The mixed multitude(Note 6) ***desired spiritual power***, so they married Abel, the royal seed of the Shekinah,(Note 10) to the .... (Read Whole Footnote in Footnote Appendix)

[62] **Blotted Out**

The day is coming, when all the thoughts of a man's heart will be judged..... (Read Whole Footnote in Footnote Appendix)

[63] **Book of Life**

The names of the people who are to inherit eternal life are written in a spiritual book called ***The Book of Life*** .... (Read Whole Footnote in Footnote Appendix)

32b You might forgive them [for making a golden calf],[64] and

32c Blot out [the judgment for] the sin [of idolatry that] is written against them] in your spiritual book," and

34a Jehovah said, "Go now, then, and lead[65] the people that belong to you [in the right path], so that

34b On the day that I told you [about,

34c When] I visit[66] [Israel] from above, to search out [the sins that the people hide behind their] personalities,[67]

---

[64] **Moses Intercedes**

The two additional energy centers that Moses received in the mount imbued him with the full power and authority of . . . . (Read Whole Footnote in Footnote Appendix)

[65] **Teach My People**

Moses is instructed to prepare the people for the day that Jehovah will reveal the hidden motives of their heart: . . . . (Read Whole Footnote in Footnote Appendix)

[66] **Motives Judged**

Jehovah knows all about the secret sins in the heart of man. They cannot be hidden from him, and he has set a time to reveal and judge them. . . . . (Read Whole Footnote in Footnote Appendix)

[67] **Hidden Sins**

Jer 17:9 – Deceitful Heart

9The heart is deceitful above all things, and . . . . (Read Whole Footnote in Footnote Appendix)

34d [The male Adam],(Note 11) the angel[68] [of the covenant that I made with Israel], shall have gone [forth to cover their inclination to do evil],"[69] and

---

[68] **Angel Of The Covenant**

The Angel of the Covenant(Note 68) stays with Israel, even when they go into captivity. . . . . (Read Whole Footnote in Footnote Appendix)

[69] **Sins Covered**

Forgiveness of sin is a process: . . . . (Read Whole Footnote in Footnote Appendix)

Hunger

For Jehovah's Words

Amos 8:11, 12-14   KJV

11 Behold, the days come, saith the Lord God,
that I will send a famine in the land,
not a famine of bread, nor a thirst for water,
but of hearing the words of the Lord:
13 And In that day shall the fair virgins and young men
faint for thirst,
14 and they that swear by the sin of Samaria, and say,
Thy [Calf] god, O Dan, liveth ....
Even they shall fall, and never rise up again.

Sowing & Reaping

35a Jehovah plagued^(Note 69) the people because

35b They married [Satan], the female power^(Note 23) [that] made [them strong enough to influence] Aaron[70] to make

35c A [golden] calf [for them],^(Note 61) and

---

[70] **Struggle For Power**

Aaron was married to the Shekinah, his spiritual covering, who made the male calf that provided Aaron with ***the spiritual power*** to rescue the people from the idolatrous male nature that had married them..... (Read Whole Footnote in Footnote Appendix)

Exodus 32:26-29

²⁶Then Moses stood in the gate of the camp, and said, Who is on the Lord 's side? let him come unto me. And all the sons of Levi gathered themselves together unto him.

²⁷And he said unto them, Thus saith the Lord God of Israel, Put every man his sword by his side, and go in and out from gate to gate throughout the camp, and slay every man his brother, and every man his companion, and every man his neighbour.

²⁸And the children of Levi did according to the word of Moses: and there fell of the people that day about three thousand men.

²⁹For Moses had said, Consecrate yourselves to day to the Lord , even every man upon his son, and upon his brother; that he may bestow upon you a blessing this day.

KJV

Moses' Prayer

---

1 Kings 18:37   KJV

37 Hear me, O Lord, hear me,
that this people may know that thou art the Lord God,
and that thou hast turned their heart back again

26a   Moses stood up(Note, 4) in the doorway⁷¹ [between the mortal and the immortal worlds], where [Satan, the female] military power(Note 23) [that married Abel(Note 61) had entered into the people], and said,

---

⁷¹   **Swinging Door**

A spiritual door, or window, separates the upper and the lower worlds..... (Read Whole Footnote in Footnote Appendix)

Two Opinions

---

1 Kings 18:21   KJV

21 And Elijah came unto all the people, and said,
How long halt ye between two opinions?
if the Lord be God, follow him:
but if Baal, then follow him.
And the people answered him not a word.

Priests Challenged

26b "The Shekinah and Jehovah are with me, all you sons of Levi, [so]

26c Depart from your [spiritual] adultery[72] [with Pharaoh,[Note 72] before Jehovah's Sowing & Reaping Judgment falls upon you]," and [then]

---

[72] **Adultery & Thigh**

Adultery – Verse 26

The Hebrew word translated *unto me*, Strong's 413, is used metaphorically to refer to sexual intercourse. . . . . (Read Whole Footnote in Footnote Appendix)

Jehovah's Fire

1 Kings 18:24   KJV

24 And call ye on the name of your gods,
and I will call on the name of the Lord:
and the God that answereth by fire, let him be God.
And all the people answered and said, It is well spoken.

Mortal Men Challenged

27a Moses said to the mortal men [who were adulterously attached to Pharaoh],

27b "Thus says Jehovah, the God of Israel,

27c 'I am bringing [Righteous Adam, my] military power[Note 9] [from [the immortal side of] the doorway,[Note 71] into the [spiritual universe[73] that your male calf] mind[Note 6] [rolled out on the mortal side of] the doorway,[Note 71] [and]

27d His drawn sword is going to slay [the male calf mind that the female power made from Abel], your [spiritual] generative part,[Note 72] and

27e [He is going to sever] Cain,[Note 6] Abel's] brother, [the conscious part of] the Evil Inclination[Note 69] which is in every mortal man, [from Leviathan],[Note 37] the companion [of Satan, the unconscious part of the Evil Inclination],[Note 69] which is in every mortal man," and

---

[73] **Spiritual Universe Of Mind**

The mind is a spiritual universe and a doorway to other spiritual worlds..... (Read Whole Footnote in Footnote Appendix)

Baal's Silence

1 Kings 18:26, 28 -29   KJV

26 And they . . . .called on the name of Baal

from morning even until noon saying,

O Baal, hear [and save] us [from the Shekinah]

28 And they cried aloud, and cut themselves after their manner

with knives and lancets, till the blood gushed out upon them.

29 and they prophesied . . .

but there was neither voice, nor any to answer, nor any that regarded.

28b The mortal men [called upon Pharaoh to save them, but he did not answer], and

28a The wisdom of [Pharaoh],(Note 72) the third [degree of] the unholy spiritual power[74] [within] the children of Levi who [abandoned their adulterous relationship with Pharaoh] when Moses told them to, fell down that day,[75] [because]

---

[74] **Illegal Spiritual Power**

Chochmah of Binah is a source of spiritual power that flows both from God, and from the **other side** .... (Read Whole Footnote in Footnote Appendix)

[75] **Walls**

Walls represent separation – something that needs to be removed..... (Read Whole Footnote in Footnote Appendix)

Seized & Slain

1 Kings 18:40

40 They seized them; and Eliyahu brought them down to Vadi Kishon

and Eliyahu killed them there.

Exodus 32:19-20, 29

¹⁹And it came to pass, as soon as he came nigh unto the camp, that he saw the calf, and the dancing: and Moses' anger waxed hot, and he cast the tables out of his hands, and brake them beneath the mount.

²⁰And he took the calf which they had made, and burnt it in the fire, and ground it to powder, and strawed it upon the water, and made the children of Israel drink of it.

²⁹For Moses had said, Consecrate yourselves to day to the Lord , even every man upon his son, and upon his brother; that he may bestow upon you a blessing this day.

KJV

The Female Power Burned

1 Kings 18:38   KJV

38 Then the fire of the Lord fell, and consumed the burnt sacrifice,
and the wood, and the stones, and the dust,
and licked up the water that was in the trench.

19a It came to pass [that], as Moses approached [the people who are Jehovah's] armies,[76] and

19b Saw the spiritual activity[(Note 27)] of the [male] calf [mind that Satan, the Serpent's female] military power,[(Note 23)] [had formed within the people who were Moses'] mate,[(Note 12)] Elohim,[(Note 50)]

20a [The Spirit within Righteous Adam,[77] the male] mind [of Moses, Jehovah's]mate,[(Note 12)] seized the [male] calf [mind that Satan, the female power],[(Note 23)] had made, and

20b The fiery stream[78] [of the Shekinah within Moses], burnt [the male calf mind[(Note 61)] that Cain, the animal side of the mixed multitude,[(Note 6)] had sacrificed Abel to make, and

---

[76] **Armies Of God**

The troops of Jehovah are the bodies that the Shekinah, the wife of the male Adam, is married to. . . . . (Read Whole Footnote in Footnote Appendix)

[77] **Moses is Adam**

Adam is the spiritual man that stands behind the human body. . . . . (Read Whole Footnote in Footnote Appendix)

[78] **Consuming Fire**

Ex 13:21 - Pillar Of Fire

The fire of God is spiritual fire: . . . . (Read Whole Footnote in Footnote Appendix)

20c The Shekinah's fiery stream](Note 78) crushed [the male calf mind,(Note 61) and

20d The five male sefirot of the female Adam] separated[79] from [Pharaoh, and

---

[79] **Separation**

The Threshing floor crushes the grain and separates the wheat from the inedible chaff. . . . . (Read Whole Footnote in Footnote Appendix)

Seed & Water

---

1 Kings 18:30   KJV

30 And Elijah said unto all the people, Come near unto me.
And all the people came near unto him.
And he repaired the altar of the Lord that was broken down

20e Moses] spread the [royal female] seed^(Note 10) of [the Shekinah]^(Note 11) upon [the earthen] personali-ties^(Note 34) of [the Levite priests of] Israel, His mate,^(Note 12) and

20f Gave [their earthen] bodies^(Note 41) [the Water of Life],^(Note 82) to drink, [and]

Jehovah Is God

1 Kings 18:39   KJV

*39 And when all the people saw it,
they fell on their faces: and they said,
The Lord, he is the God; the Lord, he is the God*

29a Moses,^(Note 82) the son of [Righteous Adam], told [the people of Israel, his] widowed wife,[80]

29b [That Jehovah] would, indeed, bless[81] the mortal men of [Israel with a spiritual male child, which would make them] the relatives^(Note 81) [of God], and that

29c In that day, [the Shekinah] would, fill [the people of Israel] with Living Water,[82] and that,

29d [Righteous Adam], would give [the people of Israel] the [female reproductive] seed^(Note 82) [of the Shekinah from the world] above, [which is the foundation out of which] Jehovah's male mind [springs].

---

[80] **Before His Son**

God gave his only begotten Son to be the ***male seed*** which would save the Woman from her sins, ... (Read Whole Footnote in Footnote Appendix)

[81] **Spiritual Relatives**

Sexual intimacy between close relatives is called ***incest***. . . . . (Read Whole Footnote in Footnote Appendix)

[82] **Living Water**

The ***Living Water***, or the ***Water of Life***, is **the spiritual semen** of Ze'ir Anpin, the son of Adam Kadmon, primordial human. . . . . (Read Whole Footnote in Footnote Appendix)

Exodus, Chapter 32

Alternate Translation

Fear Of Abandonment

1a Now, when Moses did not descend from the mountain [as quickly as] the people expected [him to, their hearts] fainted [from fear; and]

Emotional & Spiritual Weakness

1b They shamefully transferred their allegiance [from Moses] to Aaron, saying,

1c "We do not know what happened to this man, Moses, [who] empowered us to ascend above the spiritual [waters] of Egypt,

1d [So, you, Aaron, must be the one who is supposed] to stand up [in spiritual power] and make our bodies the chariots that carry Elohim,"

2a And Aaron said to [the people], "listen to me,

2b The mixed multitude, that idolatrous, male nature of the [Serpent's] Circular Universe, [has taken you to be his] wives, [and,

2c   Unless the spiritual military] power of [Jehovah] rescues [Abel], the royal [female] seed of the Shekinah [within you],

2d   You will be guilty of shedding the blood of [Abel all over again];" and

3a   All the people listened to what Aaron [said about their being guilty of] shedding the blood of [Abel, the Shekinah's] royal [female seed], again, and

5a   The widowed personalities of [the people repented, and Righteous Adam,

A New Nature

4a   Aaron's] splendid [spiritual] covering, interacted intimately with [Abel within the people, who] had said,

4b   "These [two men, Moses and Aaron, are] your Gods, O Israel, which brought you up above the spiritual waters of the land of Egypt," and

6a   [The people] drank [the Water of Life] from [the well of the Shekinah within Aaron], and

6b   Ate [the manna that congeals into the female Adam], who produces the lamb, which represents the neck [energy center of Righteous Adam, and

4c   Righteous Adam within Aaron], seized the [male calf] mind of [the mixed multitude within the people, and]

4d   Engraved [Abel, the spiritual side of the male calf] mind, [with the nature of Jehovah], and

4e   Shaped [Cain], the [animal side of the male calf] mind [of the people which were engraved with the nature of Jehovah, into the female Adam], and

Spiritual Sacrifices

5b When Aaron saw that Righteous Adam, the [spiritual] altar [upon which the male calf mind of the mixed multitude] is [sacrificed, was re]built [within the people],

5c Aaron called for [the people] to bring forth [the male calf mind of the mixed multitude from within themselves, so that

5d The Shekinah's fiery stream within Aaron] could crush [the male calf mind which was formed as a result of Abel's adultery with the female power], and

5e Bring the next day [of creation into existence within them], and

6c The people offered up [their male calf mind, the fruit of Abel's adultery with the female power], as a peace offering [to Jehovah], and

3b That is how [Righteous Adam], the spiritual, [military] power [of Jehovah within] Aaron, rescued [Abel, the royal female seed of the Shekinah within the people, from] the idolatrous [calf nature of the mixed multitude of the Serpent's] Circular Universe, [and after that],

5f The third day [of creation came into existence within the people, and

Aaron Mocked

6d Jehovah] married the people [again, but]

6e [Cain, the animal side of the male calf mind of the mixed multitude] rose up to mock [Aaron]

8a   Very soon [after Aaron rescued the people, and Cain, the animal side of]

8b   The male calf [mind of the mixed multitude],

8c   Sacrificed [Abel, the royal female seed of the Shekinah, to Satan, the female power], and

8d   [Satan], the female [power]

8e   Interacted intimately with [Abel, who was under Cain's influence, and

8f   Abel] submitted to

8g   [Cain, and to Satan, the female power], and that is how [Cain, the animal side of the mixed multitude],

8h   Covered [over Abel, who is engraved with Jehovah's righteous nature, and

8i   Turned [the people] away from the lifestyle [that Moses] commanded them [to follow], and

8j   The people spoke the blasphemous words [of the mixed multitude], saying,

8k   "[The male calf, mind of] these [Israelites, the fruit of the union of Abel and Satan, the female power], are your gods, O Israel, which empowered you to ascend above the spiritual [waters] of the material land of Egypt," and

Pharaoh's Neck

9a   Jehovah said to Moses, "I have looked into [the heart of] this people

7a   Which ascended above the [spiritual] waters of [the material land of] Egypt, and

9b   I see that

7b   [Satan, the female power] has married [my nature that you, Moses, formed in] them, and

9c   [Completed them, and that the people are expressing] the cruelty of [Pharaoh's] neck [energy center]," and

Completed Personalities

7c   Jehovah said to Moses, "go down to [the Circular world of the Universe of Separation], and

10a   Burn the male [calf mind that] the Serpent [formed within the people], and

10b   Complete [Cain, the personality of] the ox that is nailed to the [lower] window of [creation, and]

10c   Complete [the physical bodies of] the ox [of Israel], that great, widowed nation that is nailed to the [lower] window [of creation, so that

10d   They may remain [in the earth];" and

Blind To Sin

11a   Jehovah, the God [of Israel], said to Moses,

11b   "The personalities of my people [who] you are married to, are spiritually sick [concerning their inability to recognize their sins], and

12e   They have become] Egyptians [again], so

11c   [Satan, the expression of my] anger [and the enforcer of my righteous Sowing & Reaping Judgment], is raging against the [idolatrous, male calf] mind [of the mixed multitude within] my people, who

11d   Elohim, the great strength of my authority [in the earth, just] raised up above [the spiritual] waters of the material Land of Egypt, [and]

12a   [Their false] gods are speaking to them [saying that you,

12b   Moses], had an evil motive for bringing them out of captivity, [and that

12c   You intend] to slay them, [and]

12d   Consume their [spiritual] energy, [which is] greater than the energy of their earthen bodies,

Jehovah's Promise

13a   [But], I have remembered [my promises to] Abraham, Isaac and Israel, my servants, to whom I swore by my own self, saying,

13b   '[The female Adam, Abraham's] seed, shall increase into [many]

13c   Permanently fixed points of [spiritual] light in the heaven [of the Universe of Beriah], and

13d   They shall be [the inner dimension of the immortal], earthen [bodies] that I told [Jacob] about, [who] I gave the [royal female] seed [of the Shekinah to], and

13e   [Israel] shall possess eternal life;' and

Reprieve

12b   [That is the reason why] I am granting the repentance [to my people, that] comes from an higher [authority than that of Satan], the rage of my anger, [so that]

12c The evil [that Satan, the enforcer of the Sowing & Reaping Judgment, is devising] against my widowed people, shall be turned back;" and

14 Jehovah, breathed strongly against [Satan, the one who executes] the evil that [Jehovah] said he would do to his widowed people; and

A Spiritual Mind

15a Moses turned [toward the material world below], and

15b Went down [from the mountain of God] with two [additional spiritual grades], and

15c One [of the two is] the spiritual region [in Moses'] heart [center which is] across from the [spiritual] waters [of the material land of Egypt], and

15d The [other] one of the two [is] the spiritual mind [that resides there, which is] engraved with the spiritual [authority of] the male [Adam],

15e The [true and faithful] witness [that]

Engraved By God

16a The work of God

15f Is written

16b In the framework [of a man's heart], and [that]

16c They [who] write the writings of God [in the vernacular] are, themselves, engraved [with the nature of] the framer in the upper window [of creation]; and

Sin Recognized

17a   Joshua, [Moses' spiritual] mate, heard the loud shouts of the people [and] said to Moses,

17b   "[This] noise [is] the noise of the warlike military power [that opposes God, not the sound of people worshiping God," and]

The Second Witness

18a   The Eternal One spoke [through Moses, who is spiritually] male [to Joshua], saying,

18b   "[It is true], I hear the voice [of Abel, who] Cain defeated,

18c   Crying out [for the spiritual food that forms Adam's male [mind] within the people, even

18d   While they] are obeying the voice of [Satan], the female power," and

Inclined To Do Evil

21   Moses said to Aaron, "what sin did the people do that brought this great [judgment] upon them?" and

22a   Aaron said, "lord, [Moses], do not let your anger rise up, [because the people] are saying,

23a   'We do not know what happened to this man, Moses, [who] empowered us to ascend above the spiritual [waters] of Egypt, [so,

23b   You, Aaron, must be the one who is supposed] to stand up [in spiritual power] and make our bodies the chariots that carry Elohim,' [because]

22b   You know that the people are inclined to do evil, and

24a   I [have already] told them [that] they must throw down the gold[en calf that they made, and that]

24b   They will have to give up [the male calf mind] that [Satan, the female power], formed in them, [before they can] be circumcised in the Shekinah's fiery stream, [which

24c   Frees Abel, the Shekinah's royal female seed within them], and reforms him [into the male Adam again];" and

Bound To Pharaoh

30a   It came to pass [that] the [next] day, after [Aaron spoke to Moses, that],

Widowhood

25b   Moses saw that [Pharaoh], the enemy [of the Shekinah], had risen up [in spiritual power within the people]

25c   [Who were Aaron's spiritual mate, and made] Aaron a widow, and a laughingstock, [and that]

25a   The people were naked [because] they were no longer bound [to Jehovah], and

A Great Sin

30b   Moses said to the people, "you have sinned a great sin, so

30c   I will ascend before Jehovah [to see if], perhaps, [He will permit you] to atone for the sin of [the male calf mind that the female power formed in you]," and

Power For Themselves

31a Moses returned to Jehovah, and said, "Alas, the people have sinned a great sin:

31b [These] Elohim have spun the [spiritual] gold [of the Shekinah into a source of spiritual power for] themselves;" and

33a Jehovah said, "[the people] have sinned against the Shekinah, and [according to my righteous Law],

33b They should be blotted out of my Book [of Life]," and

Moses Intercedes

32a Moses [said], "please [give me] time [to teach the people how to not sin against you, so that]

32b You might forgive them [for making a golden calf], and

32c Blot out [the judgment for] the sin [of idolatry that] is written against them] in your spiritual book," and

34a Jehovah said, "Go now, then, and lead the people that belong to you [in the right path], so that

34b On the day that I told you [about,

34c When] I visit [Israel] from above, to search out [the sins that the people hide behind their] personalities,

34d [The male Adam], the angel [of the covenant that I made with Istael], shall have gone [forth to cover their inclination to do evil]," and

Sowing & Reaping

35a Jehovah plagued the people because

35b They married [Satan], the female power [that] made [them strong enough to influence] Aaron to make

35c A [golden] calf [for them], and

26a Moses stood up in the doorway [between the mortal and the immortal worlds], where [Satan, the female] military power [that married Abel had entered into the people], and said,

Priests Challenged

26b "The Shekinah and Jehovah are with me, all you sons of Levi, [so]

26c Depart from your [spiritual] adultery [with Pharaoh, before Jehovah's Sowing & Reaping Judgment falls upon you]," and [then]

Mortal Men Challenged

27a Moses said to the mortal men [who were adulterously attached to Pharaoh],

27b "Thus says Jehovah, the God of Israel,

27c 'I am bringing [Righteous Adam, my] military power [from [the immortal side of] the doorway, into the [spiritual universe that your male calf] mind [rolled out on the mortal side of] the doorway, [and]

27d His drawn sword is going to slay [the male calf mind that the female power made from Abel], your [spiritual] generative part, [and

27e [He is going to sever] Cain, [Abel's] brother, [the conscious part of] the Evil Inclination which is in every mortal man, [from Leviathan], the companion [of Satan, the unconscious part of the Evil Inclination] which is in every mortal man," and

28b The mortal men [called upon Pharaoh to save them, but he did not answer], and

Seized & Slain

28a The wisdom of [Pharaoh], the third [degree of] the unholy spiritual power [within] the children of Levi who [abandoned their adulterous relationship with Pharaoh], as Moses told them to, fell down that day, [because]

Female Power Burned

19a It came to pass [that], as Moses approached [the people who are Jehovah's] armies, and

19b Saw the spiritual activity of the [male] calf [mind that Satan, the Serpent's female] military power, [had formed within the people who were Moses'] mate, Elohim,

20a [The Spirit within Righteous Adam, the male] mind [of Moses, Jehovah's] mate, seized the [male] calf [mind that Satan, the female power], had made, and

20b The fiery stream [of the Shekinah within Moses], burnt [the male calf mind that Cain, the animal side of the mixed multitude, had sacrificed Abe to make, and

20c The Shekinah's fiery stream] crushed [the male calf mind, and

20d The five male sefirot of the female Adam] separated from [Pharaoh, and

Seed & Water

20e Moses] spread the [royal female] seed of [the Shekinah] upon the [earthen] personalities of [the Levite priests of] Israel, His mate, and

20f Gave [their earthen] bodies, [the Water of Life] to drink, [and]

Jehovah Is God

29a Moses, the son of Righteous Adam, told [the people of Israel, his] widowed wife,

29b [That Jehovah] would, indeed, bless the mortal men of [Israel with a spiritual male child, which would make them] the relatives [of God], and that,

29c In that day, [the Shekinah] would, fill [the people of Israel] with Living Water, and [that]

29d [Righteous Adam], would give [the people of Israel] the [female reproductive] seed [of the Shekinah from the world] above, [which is the foundation out of which Jehovah's] male mind [springs].

Footnotes Appendix

Footnote # 1

1 Idolatry

Ex 20:3 – No other Gods

> ³Thou shalt have no other gods before me.
>
> KJV

Footnote # 2

2   Emotional And Spiritual Weakness

Aaron taught the people that it is possible to **unwittingly** idolize their leaders and make them objects of worship, which is spiritual adultery.

2 Kings 18:4 – Idolatry In Israel

> **3**He removed the high places, and brake the images, and cut down the groves, and brake in pieces the brasen serpent that Moses had made: *for unto those days the children of Israel did burn incense to it: and he called it Nehushtan.**
>
> KJV
>
> *   ***Nehushtan*** is a noun derived from the Hebrew word that means ***copper.*** It is used sometimes to suggest spiritual fornication with a female diety.

(See, also, Note 38.)

The people believed Aaron and accepted his teachings about repentance, spiritual warfare and overcoming the idolatrous mind of the mixed multitude.

(See, also, Vs 2b & Note 6.)

Footnote # 3

3 **Spiritual Waters**

The spiritual waters of Egypt are the Egyptian Astral Plane (unholy Yetzirah).

(See, also, Note 3)

Footnote # 4

4 **Stand up in God's power**

To stand up suggests the spiritual strength and authority of manhood.

1 Kings 19:13 – God's Power

> **13**And it was so, when Elijah heard it, that he wrapped his face in his mantle, and went out, and ***stood in the entering in of the cave***. And, behold, there came a voice unto him, and said, What doest thou here, Elijah?
>
> KJV

Eph 4:13 – God's Power

> **13**Till we all come in the unity of the faith, and of the knowledge of the Son of God, unto a perfect man, unto ***the measure of the stature of the fullness of Christ:***
>
> KJV

Footnote # 5

5 A Cart For Elohim

The animal nature generates and is in control of the body, but in the days of Messiah,* Righteous Adam, the soul of Messiah, shall make the material body into a chariot that carries deity.

(*See, also, Note 63.)

Ezek 1:7 – Body To Cart

> **7**[And Righteous Adam] corrected [Ezekiel] by reforming [Satan and the Fiery Serpent*, the inhabitants of] the two, cursed lower energy centers [within Ezekiel], into **a cart [that carries Elohim]**
>
> ATB

*Num 21:6 – Fiery Serpents

> **6**And the Lord sent fiery serpents among the people, and they bit the people; and much people of Israel died.
>
> KJV

Footnote # 6

6 **Mixed Multitude**

The Mind Of The Body

Cain and Abel are one corrupt mind called **the mixed multitude**.

The **mixed multitude** *came into existence as a result of the spiritual adultery between the female Adam and the Primordial Serpent.*

The **mixed multitude** is a Kabbalistic term for *the spiritual-mental-emotional* **nature** *called,* **beast, animal,** *or* **body**.

In the New Testament, **the mixed multitude**, is called **the Carnal Mind**.

(See, also, Note 10.)

The fiery serpent is a spiritual name for Cain.

Cain is a serpent, because his father is **the Serpent**.

Cain is the spiritual foundation of mortal man.

Lk 14:29 - Foundation

> **29**Lest haply, after he hath laid the **foundation**, and is not able to finish it, all that behold it begin to mock him,
>
> KJV

The mind of mortal man is called **the Carnal Mind**.

The Carnal Mind is the **lower mind** of the animal nature of mortal man.

Rom 1:28 – Reprobate Mind

28And even as they did not like to retain God in their knowledge, God gave them over to ***a reprobate mind***, to do those things which are not convenient;

KJV

Rom 8:7 – Carnal Mind

7Because ***the carnal mind is enmity against God***: for it is not subject to the law of God, neither indeed can be.

KJV

Two Seeds

The woman has two offspring, one from each of her two husbands.

Cain is the Serpent's seed.

Abel is Adam's seed.

Abel is the female seed of Righteous Adam.

Abel was in Adam's loins when Adam fell asleep.

Abel is sleeping, and does not remember who he is.

The male Adam is sent to rouse Abel from the sleep of death.

Cain guards Abel to prevent his spiritual awakening.

1 Cor 15:34 – Awake To Righteousness

34*Awake to righteousness*, and sin not; for some have not the knowledge of God . . . .

KJV

Rom 13:11 – Awake Out Of Sleep

11And that, knowing the time, that now it is high time to **awake out of sleep**: for now is our salvation nearer than when we believed.

KJV

The **Doctrine of Christ** and **Christ-Centered Kabbalah** call Righteous Adam **Christ Jesus.**

(See, also, Note 11.)

Cain and Abel Are Mortal enemies

Gen 4:1-2 – Cain & Abel

1And **Adam knew Eve his wife**; and she conceived, **and bare Cain**, and said, I have gotten a man from the Lord.

2And she **again bare his brother Abel**. And Abel was a keeper of sheep, but Cain was a tiller of the ground.

KJV

Gen 3:14-15 – The Serpent

14And the **Lord God said unto the serpent**, Because thou hast done this, **thou art cursed above all cattle**, and above every beast of the field; upon thy belly shalt thou go, and dust shalt thou eat all the days of thy life:

15And *I will put enmity between thee and the woman*, and **between thy seed and her seed**; it shall bruise thy head, and thou shalt bruise his heel.

KJV

(See, also, Notes 10, 11.)

Footnote # 7

7 **Circular Universe**

The universe that we live in and are familiar with is circular, but there is also a linear universe called ***the Image of God***. (Wilder & Padeh, *Tree of Life: The Palace of Adam Kadmon* (Jason Aronson Inc., 1999) pp. 19-24.)

Footnote # 8

8   **Spiritual Wives**

A personality can be bonded, or married to God, or to a spirit, either directly, or indirectly through another man.

Moses was bonded to Jehovah, and the people were bonded to Jehovah through their soul tie with Moses. (See, also, Note 41).

1 Cor 10:2-4 – In The Cloud

2And [they] were all baptized unto Moses in the cloud and in the sea;

3And did all eat the same spiritual meat;

4And did all drink the same spiritual drink: for they drank of that spiritual Rock that followed them: and that Rock was Christ.

KJV

Rom 7:4 – Spiritual Husband

4 Wherefore, my brethren, ye also are become dead to the law by the body of Christ; that **ye should be married to another, even to him who is raised from the dead**, that we should bring forth fruit unto God.

KJV

(See, also, Note 25.)

Footnote # 9

9 The Military Power of Jehovah

Jehovah's warfare is in the spiritual plane.

The visible world is an aspect, or a reflection, of the spiritual world. It does not have its own reality.

Everything that happens in the spiritual plane, affects, and is revealed through, the visible world.

Deut 1:30 - He Shall Fight For You

> **30**The Lord your God which goeth before you, **he shall fight for you**, according to all that he did for you in Egypt before your eyes;
>
> KJV

Isa 27:1 – Spiritual Sword

> **1**In that day the Lord with his sore and great and strong sword shall punish leviathan the piercing serpent, even leviathan that crooked serpent; and **he shall slay the** dragon **that is in the sea.**
>
> KJV

2 Cor 10:4 – Spiritual Weapons

> **4**(*For the weapons of our warfare are not carnal*, but mighty through God to the pulling down of strong holds;)
>
> KJV

Footnote # 10

10 **Royal Female Seed**

Abel is the Shekinah in captivity, the female seed that has the potential to mature into the male calf mind that joins the Earth of humanity to the Heavenly worlds.

Matt 13:24 - Seed

> **24**Another parable put he forth unto them, saying, ***The kingdom of heaven is likened unto a man which sowed good seed*** in his field:
>
> KJV

(See, also, Rev 12:4-5, Note 12.)

Abel is the beginning, or the first, of the 10 Sefirot of the regenerating female Adam in a mortal man. (See, Appendix 1, p. 197)

Abel joined to his Mother is called ***the Shekinah***.

(See, also, Note 11.)

Footnote # 11

11 **The Shekinah**

There is a Shekinah above and a Shekinah below.

The Shekinah above is called ***Mother/Understanding***.

The Shekinah below is called

Abel , or

The Shekinah in captivity . . .

. . . when she is separated from her Mother.

The Shekinah below is called ***Elohim*** . . .

. . . when she and her mother are one.

John 10:30 – One Soul

30I and my Father are one.

KJV

The Shekinah in the earth is called ***a hart*** or ***a gazelle***, because her existence is rooted in the animal body.

Ps 42:1 – A Female Deer

1As ***the hart*** panteth after the water brooks, so panteth my soul after thee, O God.

KJV

Soncino Zohar, Bereshith, Section 1, Page 4a

. . . [T]he King visits each day and remembers ***his gazelle*** which is trodden in the dust . . . .

The Shekinah's Son

The Shekinah's mazel, or destiny, is to produce a spiritual son who will join Heaven and Earth, the upper and lower worlds.

The Shekinah in the earth is a seed called **Abel**.

Abel has a male side, his six sub-sefirot, from Yesod through Chesed.

The Shekinah (Abel's) male side (the collective six sefirot) is called a [spiritual] ***calf*** (mind).

Rev 4:7 – A Spiritual Calf Mind

> ⁷ And the first beast was like a lion, and the second beast like a calf, and the third beast had a face as a man, and the fourth beast was like a flying eagle. KJV

The Shekinah (Abel's) <u>completed</u> male side is called a [spiritual] ***male calf*** (mind).

The Shekinah (Abel's) <u>incomplete</u> male side is called a [spiritual] ***female calf*** (mind).

The Shekinah from above, completes **the Shekinah (Abel)**, the [spiritual] female calf (mind), below.

The completed [spiritual] ***calf*** (mind), **which is now male,** is called **the son of the Shekinah,** or **the son of the woman.** (See, Rev. 4:12, below.)

The son of the Shekinah is a soul that is likened to a spiritual calf (mind) (see, Rev 4:7, 12, above).

Metatron is the ***awakened Abel***, the female calf (mind) of the Shekinah. He is called ***lad***, or, ***young man*** in the Zohar.

Soncino Zohar, Bereshith, Section 1, Page 237b

> JUDAH IS A LION'S WHELP: first he will be a whelp, and then a lion, corresponding to the transition from "lad" [tr.note: i.e. Metatron.] to "man," as it is written: "The Lord is a man of war" (Ex. xv, 3).

Reiteration

> At first he is ***Abel***, a humble seed; after that he is awakened, ***Metatron***, a fledging female calf

emerges which has the potential to mature into the **Lamb of God,** the Shekinah's mature son . . . .

Metatron has the potential to mature into the male Adam, the spiritual bridge that connects Heaven and Earth.

Metatron in the New Testament is called **Christ.**

New Testament Definitions

Christ Jesus is the bridge that connects Heaven (the God world of Atzilut) and Earth (humanity).

1 Tim 2:5 – Only One Mediator

> 5For there is one God, and ***one mediator between God and men, the man Christ Jesus***;
>
> KJV

Christ Jesus is the personification of the ladder, or staircase, that connects the two worlds.

Gen 28:12 - Ladder To Heaven

> 12He dreamt that there before him was a ladder resting on the ground with its top reaching to heaven, and the angels of *Ad-nai* were going up and down on it.
>
> KJV

The Lord Jesus Christ is the garment that dresses Ancient Adam (Adam Kadmon), the only one who is truly alive.

The spiritual office of the Lord Jesus Christ can be likened to the worldly office of Joseph, Viceroy of all Egypt, who was second only to Pharaoh.

The attributes and actions of the Lord Jesus Christ express the Will of Ancient Adam (Adam Kadmon). He has no attributes and does not engage in any activities.

The Lord Jesus Christ relates to humanity from the grade of Mother/Understanding of the God world of Atzilut.

Christ is the name of the Shekinah in captivity, when she is separated from her mother, the Shekinah above.

The Lamb of God is the mature son of the Shekinah.

Christ Jesus is the Lamb of God.

The marriage of the Lord Jesus Christ (from the grade of **Mother**) in Heaven, to Christ Jesus (his own son in the earth of humanity), joins Heaven (the God world of Atzilut) and Earth (humanity).

Footnote # 12

12 Spiritual Marriage

An intimacy, or spiritual marriage, can exist between two men. It can also exist between a teacher and his disciples.

2 Sam 1:26 – Passing The Love Of Women

> **26**I am distressed for thee, my brother Jonathan: very pleasant hast thou been unto me: **thy love to me was wonderful, passing the love of women.**
>
> KJV

In this context, it can be said that:

Moses was the husband of the people that he led out of Egypt,

The people were Moses' spiritual wife, and

Moses' spiritual wife was widowed when she believed that Moses would never return.

(See, also, Note 51.)

Rom 7:4 – Married to Christ

> **4**Wherefore, my brethren, ye also are become dead to the law by the body of Christ; that **ye should be married to another, even to him who is raised from the dead**, that **we should bring forth fruit unto God**.
>
> KJV

The body must be married to a spiritual (inner) man to exist in this world.

Eph 3:16 – Inner Man

> **16** That he would grant you, according to the riches of his glory, to be strengthened with might by his Spirit in the inner man;
>
> KJV

Cain is the spiritual foundation and husband of the bodies of the mortal men of humanity.

(See, also, Note 6, ***Two seeds***.)

The personality is the spiritual dimension of the body.

Leviathan, Cain's father, is the spiritual husband of every personality born of a woman, except those who are married to the Lord Jesus Christ.

God would have us all to bear his son, Christ Jesus, the bride of the Lord Jesus Christ.

Rev 12:4-5 – A Male Child

> **4** And . . . . the dragon stood before the woman which was ready to be delivered, for ***to devour her child as soon as it was born.***
>
> **5** And ***she brought forth a man child***, who was to rule all nations with a rod of iron: and her child was caught up unto God, and to his throne.
>
> KJV

(See, also, Notes 11, ***the Shekinah's Son***, and 13.)

Footnote # 13

13 **Righteous Adam**

Righteous Adam is the regenerated Adam who died.

Righteous Adam is the only Son of his mother, the Shekinah above.

The Shekinah has a male seed – the seed of her unborn son.

The male seed of the Shekinah is the sperm of the spiritual semen of Jehovah.

The spiritual semen of Jehovah is called the ***Water of Life*** (***Living Water***).

(See, also, Note 14.)

The unmarried male Adam lives in the world above, and must have a home below, a pillow in the earth to lay his head upon, to bridge the two worlds (Heaven and Earth).

Matt 8:20 – No Pillow

> 20And Jesus saith unto him, The foxes have holes, and the birds of the air have nests; but the Son of man hath not where to lay his head.
>
> KJV

The male Adam marries the female Adam (the Shekinah below) (Old Testament), or Christ Jesus (New Testament).

The Shekinah is the male Adam's pillow.

The unity of Heaven and Earth, male and female, is also known as

> ***Ze'ir Anpin and Nukvah, the married couple***
>
> ***The spiritual Sabbath***
>
> ***The higher soul of Israel***.

Righteous Adam is the soul of Moshiach (Messiah).

Isa 9:6 – A Child Is Born

⁶For ***a child is born to us, a son is given to us***; dominion will rest on his shoulders, and he will be given the name Pele-Yo'etz El Gibbor Avi-'Ad Sar-Shalom [Wonder of a Counselor, Mighty God, Father of Eternity, Prince of Peace].

KJV

The married male Adam compasses all four worlds:

Atzilut, the World of Emanation (the power of God goes forth from here);

Beriah, the World of Creation (the Mind of God, or the Mental Plane);

Yetzitah, the World of Formation (primitive forms appear here);

Asiyah, the World of Action (the Will of God is acted out here);

His ***head*** is in Atzilut;

His ***heart*** is in Beriah;

His ***feet*** are in Yetzirah;

His ***image*** is in the mind of Israel;

His ***footsteps*** are the bodies of Jacob.

Ze'ir Anpin is Heaven.

The Shekinah is the Earth.

The Shekinah is married to the personalities of Israel.

(See, also, Note 8.)

Gen 1:1 - Heaven & Earth

1In the beginning *God created the heavens and the earth.*

KJV

Footnote # 14

14 Well of Existence

The Shekinah is called a Well because she is spiritually equipped to receive, contain and propagate the ***Water of Life***.

She is called ***the Well of Existence***, or ***the Well of Life***, because she is the only source of Life in the lower world. (See, also, Note 11.)

John 4:11 – Living Water

> **11**The woman saith unto him, Sir, thou hast nothing to draw with, and ***the well is deep: from whence then hast thou that living water***?
>
> KJV

John 7:38 – Rivers Of Living Water

> **38**He that believeth on me, as the scripture hath said, ***out of his belly shall flow rivers of living water***.
>
> KJV

The Shekinah has no light of her own, but is called ***the Light of the World***, because she reflects the Light of Ancient Adam (Kadmon), primordial human.

John 9:5 – Jesus, Light Of The World

> **5**As long as I am in the world, I am the light of the world.
>
> KJV

Matt 5:14 – Light Of The World

14 Ye are the light of the world. A city that is set on an hill cannot be hid.

KJV

Ancient Adam (Adam Kadmon) is the Living One, the only one who is truly alive.

Ancient Adam (Adam Kadmon)*,* primordial human, incarnated as Elijah, Moses and as Jesus of Nazareth,

The name, ***the Lord Jesus Christ***, is inclusive of all three spiritual men.

(See, also, Note 11.)

Quantum theory says that ***man creates his own reality, because the observer influences the outcome***.

In other words, if there are three possibilities, the possibility that the observer ***looks at,*** becomes the reality.

Spiritually speaking, then, the individual experiences ***the first day of creation*** when the Living One ***looks at*** him, or ***remembers him***, or ***becomes aware that he exists***.

The Water of Life that goes forth from ***that look,**** carries the male seed that grafts to Abel, the Shekinah in captivity, the female seed that is joined to the body from birth, and provides the personality with the potential to become ***a Well of Torah knowledge***.

(See, also, Notes 11, 34.)

> *** Rabbi Gedaliah HaLevi*** describes how ***the look from the eyes of Adam Kadmo***n formed the vessels which were to be infused with the Light of the Ayn Sof. (Wilder & Padeh, *Tree of Life: The Palace of Adam Kadmon* (Jason Aronson Inc., 1999) pp. 122-125.)

On the other hand, the ***Shekinah in captivity*** must first ***see,**** or become aware, that this Living Water (spiritual sperm) exists, before she can be filled with the life of her betrothed.

(See, also, Note 82.)

Soncino Zohar, Bereshith, Section 1, Page 135b

It is written: A fountain of gardens, a well of living waters, and flowing streams from Lebanon (S. S. IV, 1).

"A fountain of gardens" is a description of Abraham;

"A well of living waters" is a description of Isaac, of whom it is written: "And Isaac dwelt by the well of the living and seeing one (beer-lahai-roi)."

The "well" is none other but the Shekinah;

(See, also, Note 11.)

"The living waters" is an allusion to t**he Righteous One who lives in the two worlds**, that is, who lives above, in the higher world, and who also lives in the lower world, which exists and is illumined through him, just as the moon is only illumined when she looks at the sun.

(See, also, Note 13.)

Thus the well of existence literally emanates from "the living waters" whom "it sees", and when it looks at him it is filled with living waters.

(See, also, Note 82.)

Footnote # 15

15 Manna Is Spiritual Food

Manna is spiritual food. God's people in the wilderness missed the physical and emotional comforts of Egypt, as well as Egyptian mystery religion, so Jehovah sent manna from heaven to nourish and sustain them in the wilderness.

Ex 16:15 – What Is It?

15And when the children of Israel saw it, they said one to another, *It is manna: for they wist not what it was*. And Moses said unto them, *This is the bread which the Lord hath given you to eat.*

KJV

Soncino Zohar, Shemoth, Section 2, Page 183b

Therefore, when He gave the Torah to Israel He gave them to taste of that **supernal bread of the celestial realm, namely, the manna, by means of which they were enabled to perceive and penetrate into the mysteries of the Torah and to walk in the straight path.**

John 6:58 – Heavenly Manna

58This is that bread which came down from heaven: *not as your fathers did eat manna, and are dead*: he that eateth of this bread shall live forever.

KJV

Rev 2:17 – Hidden Manna

17He that hath an ear, let him hear what the Spirit saith unto the churches; *To him that*

***overcometh will I give to eat of the hidden manna**, and will give him a white stone, and in the stone a new name written, which no man knoweth saving he that receiveth it.*

   KJV

Footnote # 16

16 Manna, The Flesh Of The Shekinah

Manna is the spiritual food that restores the broken relationship between Abel, the Shekinah in captivity, and the Shekinah above.

Manna nourishes the regenerating female Adam, and equips her to produce the female calf (mind) that connects the Earth to the Heavenly worlds.

(See, also, Note 11.)

Soncino Zohar, Bemidbar, Section 3, Page 155b

> NOW THE MANNA WAS LIKE CORIANDER (gad) SEED. Said R. Jose:
>
> The term "gad" (lit. troops) signifies that ***the manna had the virtue of inducing propagation.*** It implies further that in the same way as the seed of Gad took their portion in another land, [Tr. note: i.e. outside the border of the Holy Land proper, in Transjordania.] so ***the manna*** hovered over Israel outside the Holy Land.
>
> We may also explain the words to mean that it was white [holy] in appearance, like coriander seed, and ***coagulated*** when it reached the atmosphere, ***and was transmuted into material substance***: [Tr. note: i.e. out of its ethereal state.] inside the body. [Tr. note: Al. "it was absorbed by the body", i.e. without leaving any waste, as with material food. v. T.B. Yoma, 75b.]

John 1:14 – Spiritual Flesh

14And ***the Word was made flesh***, and dwelt among us, (and we beheld his glory, the glory as of the only begotten of the Father), full of grace and truth.

KJV

AND THE APPEARANCE THEREOF AS THE APPEARANCE OF BDELLIUM, to wit, IT WAS WHITE IN COLOUR LIKE BDELLIUM, THIS BEING THE COLOUR OF THE RIGHT IN THE SUPERNAL SPHERE.

Abel, the Shekinah in captivity, is the seed of faith that roots in the mind and matures into the female Adam (the Shekinah).

(See, also, Notes 10, 12.)

The Word of God is the vehicle that carries the seed.

1 Cor 1:21 – Foolishness Of Preaching

21For after that in the wisdom of God the world by wisdom knew not God, it pleased God by the foolishness of preaching to save them that believe.

KJV

A Parable Of The Seeds

Cain represents the ground, or the mind, that the seed of the higher mind is planted in.

Abel, the seed out of which the female calf (mind) eventually emerges, is willing to die so that the male calf (mind) that connects the two worlds, can come into existence.

(See, also, Note 11.)

Jehovah rejected Cain's offering because the earth alone, without a seed, cannot produce the male calf (mind) that Jehovah desires.

(See, also, Note 82.)

Gen 4:3-4 – The Lord Accepts Abel

> **3**And in process of time it came to pass, that Cain brought of the fruit of the ground an offering unto the Lord.
>
> **4**And Abel, he also brought of the firstlings of his flock and of the fat thereof. ***And the Lord had respect unto Abel and to his offering:***
>
> KJV

(See, also, Notes 6, 10.)

Cain thought that, since Abel was going to die anyway, he might as well pick the time and use Abel's death to his own advantage.

King David had a similar thought when he took Bathsheba before the appointed time.

David knew that Bathsheba was to be his wife, and that she would bear Solomon, the son out of which the kings of Judah would emerge.

Jehovah surely would have dealt with the problem of Uriah in his own way, and in his own time, but David took matters into his own hands.

2 Sam 12:9-10 – Uriah

> **9**Wherefore hast thou despised the commandment of the Lord, to do evil in his sight? ***thou hast killed Uriah the Hittite*** with the sword, and hast taken his wife to be thy wife, and hast slain him with the sword of the children of Ammon.

10Now therefore the sword shall never depart from thine house; because ***thou hast despised me, and hast taken the wife of Uriah the Hittite to be thy wife***.

KJV

Footnote # 17

17 The Neck Of Righteous Adam

The neck of Righteous Adam is called *the Lamb*.

The neck of Righteous Adam is the point where the upper and lower worlds, Heaven and Earth, meet.

The neck of Righteous Adam joins the female Adam below and the God world of Atzilut above.

(See, also, Notes 11,13.)

The Lamb, *the neck of Righteous Adam*, comes into existence when Malchut of the higher world joins with Chesed, the fifth of the five male Sefirot produced by the regenerated female Adam in a human.

Chesed of the female Adam channels the *compassion* of the Keter from the world above to the female Adam below, and to the physical body, through a knowledge of the mysteries of the Word of God (Torah).

In this capacity, the neck of Righteous Adam becomes the channel to *the throne of God*, the vessel that Jehovah and the other Names of God descend into and rest in.

Should an unholy (male) calf (mind) come into existence (rather than a Lamb) because of spiritual adultery between an Israelite and an unholy spirit, the neck of the calf (mind) must be broken to separate the five sefirot of the female Adam from the unholy male seed.

The Law of National Israel calls for the neck of a female cow (representing the animal nature of the guilty parties) to be broken to atone for the spiritual adultery that produced the male calf (mind).

(See, Vs 2b, 7b, 9c.)

Deut 21:1, 4 – Break Its Neck

1If ***one be found slain in the land*** which the Lord thy God giveth thee to possess it, lying in the field, and it be not known who hath slain him:

4The leaders of that town are to bring the heifer down to a vadi with a stream in it that never dries up, to a place that is neither plowed nor sown; and ***they are to break the cow's neck*** there in the vadi.

KJV

But Moses used spiritual power to liberate the captured Israelites.

(See, also, Vs 20 & Note 79.)

Soncino Zohar, Bereshith, Section 1, Page 114a

"***If one be found slain in the land***, etc." (Deut. XXI, 1-9). Ordinarily it is through the angel of death that the souls of men pass out of their bodies, but with that man it was not so, but he that slew him made his soul depart from him before the time came for the angel of death to gather him in.

Hence it is written: "***And no expiation can be made for the land for the blood that is shed therein, but by the blood of him that shed it***" (Num. XXXV, 33).

Is it not enough for the world that Satan should be continually on the watch to lead men astray and to formulate accusations against them, that one must needs increase his fury by depriving him of what is his due?

But the Holy One is merciful towards His children, and so provided ***the offering of a calf***

> *as reparation for the soul of which Satan was deprived and as a means of pacifying the world's accuser.*
>
> Herein is involved a deep mystery. The offerings of the ox, the cow, the calf, the heifer have all a deep mystical significance, and therefore we make reparation to him in the way mentioned in the text.
>
> Hence the declaration, "***Our hands have not shed this blood**, etc.*" (Deut. XXI, 7)- ***they have not shed this blood, and we have not caused his death***; and by this means the accuser is thereby kept at a distance. All this constitutes good counsel given by the Holy One to the world.

A female calf is sacrificed instead of shedding the blood of the murderer.

The heifer's shed blood also frees the local elders from their responsibility to execute the guilty party.

The neck of the female calf is broken with a hatchet, signifying that the power of the unholy male calf over the townspeople is broken.

The soul of Elijah within Jesus broke the neck of the unholy calf (mind) that joined Jesus' soul to his body, thus, separating Jesus' soul from the marrow of his bones, and his human spirit from Satan, the spiritual ruler of the house.

(See, also, Heb 4:12, Note 79.)

Heb 4:12 – A Broken Neck

> **12** For the word of God is quick, and powerful, and sharper than any twoedged sword, piercing even to the dividing asunder of soul and spirit, and of the joints and marrow, and is

a discerner of the thoughts and intents of the heart.

KJV

Footnote # 18

18 **Engraving Tool**

The nature, or character, of a person reveals the source of their spirit.

Spiritually speaking, mind is likened to stone, so one's nature is said to be ***engraved***.

Ezek 9:4 – Mark of God

4And the Lord said unto him, Go through the midst of the city, through the midst of Jerusalem, and ***set a mark upon the foreheads of the men that sigh and that cry for all the abominations that be done*** in the midst thereof.

KJV

Phil 3:14 – Mark of God

14I press toward ***the mark for the prize of the high calling*** *of God* in Christ Jesus.

KJV

Footnote # 19

19 **Formed From The Dust**

Jehovah's breath engraves his nature on the soul of man.

Gen 2:7 – Shaped

7And the Lord ***God formed man of the dust of the ground***, and breathed into his nostrils the breath of life; and man became a living soul.

KJV

John 5:37 – Mind Shaped

37And the Father himself, which hath sent me, hath borne witness of me. ***Ye have neither*** heard his voice at any time, nor ***seen his shape***.

KJV

(See, also, Note 18.)

Footnote # 20

20 The End Of The Transgression

The soul of fallen mankind is a chameleon. It changes from righteous to evil and from evil to righteous; depending on the higher soul that controls it.

Jehovah has promised, however, to bring this unstable soul to an end, and to establish mankind in a permanent state of righteousness, through marriage to the Righteous One.

Dan 9:24 – Eternal Righteousness

> **24** Seventy weeks are determined upon thy people and upon thy holy city, to finish the transgression, and to make an end of sins, and to make reconciliation for iniquity, and to bring in everlasting righteousness, and to seal up the vision and prophecy, and to anoint the most Holy.
>
> KJV

Reiteration

24 Jehovah has decreed that the whole animal shall depart from this perverse age and enter into **the age of eternal righteousness** through union with the male Adam,[Note 13] her true husband, and

[Righteous Adam][Note 13] shall engrave[Note 18] Jehovah's nature upon the woman, which will end the adultery,[Notes 6, 38] and

The spirit of Elijah shall expand into the many members of the whole beast, and raise the female seed[Note 10] of the Shekinah, the female Adam,[Note 11] from the dead, in each individual, and

The Shekinah, the female Adam, shall **scab over [Cain, Abel's wound]**,[Note 52] and Righteous Adam[Note

13) shall restrain the rebellious Serpent, and the woman shall experience the end of the ages.

ATB

(See, also, Note 41.)

Matt 11:14 - Elias

14 And if ye will receive it, this is Elias, which was for to come.

KJV

Footnote # 21

21 Spiritual Altar

The female Adam (Christ Jesus in the New Testament) is the spiritual altar of God, the place where the unholy male calf (mind) of the mixed multitude is sacrificed.

Heb 13:8 – Our Altar

> ¹We have an altar, whereof they have no right to eat which serve the tabernacle.
>
> KJV

Rev 6:9 – Under The Altar

> ⁹And when he had opened the fifth seal, I saw **under the altar** the souls of them that were slain for the word of God, and for the testimony which they held:
>
> KJV

(See, also, Notes 6, 13, 61)

Righteous Adam, kills and breaks apart the unholy male calf, (mind) joins with the Shekinah's female calf (mind), and forms a male calf (mind) in his own image.

Fire is the agent that kills and breaks apart the sacrifice:

Ex 30:19-20

> ¹⁹For Aaron and his sons shall wash their hands and their feet thereat:
>
> ²⁰When they go into the tabernacle of the congregation, they shall wash with water, that they die not; or when they come near to the altar to minister, **to burn offering made by fire unto the Lord** :
>
> KJV

(See, also, Vs 20, Notes 13)

In this context, **Righteous Adam** is Jehovah's spiritual High Priest.

Heb 3:1 – High Priest

> **1**Wherefore, holy brethren, partakers of the heavenly calling, consider the Apostle and **High Priest of our profession, Christ Jesus**;
>
> KJV

Heb 4:14 – Into The Heavens

> **14**Seeing then that we have *a great high priest*, that is passed into the heavens, *Jesus the Son of God*, let us hold fast our profession.
>
> KJV

Footnote # 22

22 Male Calf

Footnote 11, The Shekinah, and *The Female Calf,* introduce the following subject matter.

The **male calf** (mind) is the spiritual zygote formed from the female calf (mind) of the Shekinah, and a male seed.

The male seed is carried to the Shekinah's female calf (mind) either by the Living Water[Note 82] of Adam Kadmon, primordial human, or by the male water of the female power.

The mature male calf (mind) appears in the Universe of Beriah as **a ram**, whose spiritual DNA is **an exact copy** of the spiritual DNA of Ze'ir Anpin of Atzilut.[Note 11]

Dan 8:3 – A Ram

> ³Then I lifted up mine eyes, and saw, and, behold, there stood before the river **a ram which had two horns**: and the two horns were high; but one was higher than the other, and the higher came up last.
>
> KJV

Faith, the highest of the three heads of the Keter, the super conscious, contains the spiritual DNA of the world above. One of the functions of this head is to superimpose the DNA of the higher world upon the lower world.

Adam Kadmon, primordial human, passes his spiritual DNA to the Keter of Atzilut, who passes it to the Father (Chochmah) of Atzilut, where it becomes seed.

The Father, then, passes his genetically engraved seed to Ze'ir Anpin, the Son of God in the World of Atzilut, where it becomes spiritual sperm in his Yesod.

After that, **Ze'ir Anpin** passes his spiritual sperm to Nukvah, his wife, who, in turn, pours it out upon the Shekinah below, the female Adam, who has risen up into Beriah from the depths of the sea.

(See, Note 11.)

Ps 68:22 – I Will Fetch Them

22The Lord said, I will bring again from Bashan, *I will bring my people again from the depths of the sea:*

KJV

The female Adam is the foundation of the reconstructed Righteous Adam,

The male calf (mind) that comes into existence after that, unifies the two worlds, Atzilut and Beriah, the world of Creation.

The female calf (mind) is the upper edge of the lower world, Beriah, and the male seed is the lower edge of the world above.

The female calf (mind) is **the marriage bed**, the place of union of the two Adams.

The male calf (mind) is inclusive of the female calf (mind). It is the channel to **the Throne of God**.

The male calf (mind) is also **the neck of Righteous Adam**.

Adam Kadmon, primordial human, is marrying the regenerated female Adam, in the midst of the physical bodies of Israel.

The union is male to male.

The World of Beriah must be reconstructed, because it is the foundation upon which **the World of Rectification** is built.

The World of Rectification is the Mind of Christ.

The World of Rectification defends the female Adam against the shells.

(See, *Standing Against the Outsiders*, Wilder & Padeh, *Tree of Life: The Palace of Adam Kadmon* (Jason Aronson Inc., 1999) pp. 242-243.)

(See, Appendix 5, The Primeval Worlds, p 121.)

(See, also, Note 11.)

There is a ***calf*** In the New Testament.:

Rev 4:7 – New Testament Calf

> **7**And the first beast was like a lion, ***and the second beast like a calf***, and the third beast had a face as a man, and the fourth beast was like a flying eagle.
>
> KJV

There is also a ***Lamb:***

The Lamb is the mind that produces the promised sinless nature.

John 1:36 – Christ Jesus Is The Lamb

> **36**And looking upon Jesus as he walked, he saith, ***Behold the Lamb of God!***
>
> KJV

1 John 2:2 – The Sins Of The World

> **2*****And he is the propitiation for*** our sins: and not for ours only, but also for ***the sins of the whole world.***

Rev 7:17 – Lamb In The Midst

> **17**For ***the Lamb which is in the midst of the throne*** shall feed them, and shall lead them

unto living fountains of waters: and God shall wipe away all tears from their eyes.

KJV

The spiritual Blood of Jesus will overshadow and replace the blood of fallen Adam in the physical bodies of humanity.

Rev 12:11 – Blood Of The Lamb

11And ***they overcame him by the blood of the Lamb***, and by the word of their testimony; and they loved not their lives unto the death.

KJV

Rev 19:7 – The Lamb's Wife

7Let us be glad and rejoice, and give honour to him: for ***the marriage of the Lamb is come***, and ***his wife hath made herself ready***.

KJV

Footnote # 23

23 The Female Power

God is in full control of all of the events in the earth.

All power and authority belong to, and go forth from God, who is male.

The visible world is not yet reconciled with God's reality, however, so it appears to those who are bound here, that there is another power.

The difficulty for the natural man is his inability, or unwillingness, to believe that a righteous God could be responsible for the pain experienced in this world.

The truth is, however, that Satan, the female enforcer of Jehovah's righteous Sowing & Reaping Judgment, is Jehovah's faithful and obedient servant.

Dan 11:38 – The Female Power

> 38But in his estate shall he honour the [female] God of forces: and a god whom his fathers knew not shall he honour with gold, and silver, and with precious stones, and pleasant things.
>
> KJV

Rom 13:1 – No Power, But God

> 37Let every soul be subject unto the higher powers. For **there is no power but of God**: the powers that be are ordained of God.
>
> KJV

24 Grass

Grass is a symbol for the female Adam [Note 11] who appeared on the third day of creation.

Gen 1:12-13 - Third Day

12 ***And the earth brought forth grass***, and herb yielding seed after his kind, and the tree yielding fruit, whose seed was in itself, after his kind: and God saw that it was good.

13 And the evening and the morning were ***the third day***.

KJV

1 Cor 15:4 – Third Day

4 And that he was buried, and that ***he rose again the third day*** according to the scriptures:

KJV

Footnote # 25

25 Bonded To Jehovah

The people who were bonded to Jehovah through their **spiritual marriage** (Note 12) to Moses, lost both spiritual unions when they **divorced Moses** in their hearts.(Note 12)

But Aaron married his brother, Moses', spiritual widow, in accordance with the Levirate Law. After that, the people were joined to Jehovah again through their spiritual marriage to Aaron.

Deut 25:5 – Levirate Marriage

5 If brethren dwell together, and one of them die, and have no child, the wife of the dead shall not marry without unto a stranger: her husband's brother shall go in unto her, and take her to him to wife, and perform the duty of an husband's brother unto her.

KJV

Col 2:10 - Complete

10And **ye are complete in him**, which is the head of all principality and power:

KJV

Footnote # 26

26 Spiritual Arrogance

The second time the people sinned, they were no longer naïve and ignorant.

This time they **sinned with knowledge**, believing that they were wiser than their teacher.

Acts 13:8 - Elymas

> **8**But Elymas the sorcerer (for so is his name by interpretation) withstood them, **seeking to turn away the deputy from the faith.**
>
> KJV

They rejected Aaron's wisdom and authority, were tricked into marrying the female power,[Note 23] and were wholly overtaken by the idolatrous mind and emotions of the material body, their lower nature.

Song 5:4, 6 – Seduction & Ruin

> **4**My beloved put in his hand by the hole of the door, and my bowels were moved for him.
>
> **6**I opened to my beloved; but my beloved had withdrawn himself, and was gone: my soul failed when he spake: *I sought him, but I could not find him; I called him, but he gave me no answer.*
>
> KJV

The first sin was the fruit of emotional and spiritual weakness.

The second sin was the fruit of spiritual arrogance.

Sometimes spiritual children think that they are above the teachers who restrained them in their youth.

Spiritual arrogance is a danger for both natural and spiritual children.

Hopefully, the wisdom previously taught becomes a personal ***discovery,*** and ***freedom through self-imposed restraint,*** the middle ground between authoritative control and anarchy, is attained.

(See, also, Note 1.)

Footnote # 27

267 Cuckold

A cuckold is an object of scorn because a man's wife took a lover. The suggestion is that the man could not satisfy her.

The people were not satisfied with having their sin nature revealed. They desired greater degrees of spirituality than Aaron offered them.

Heb 10:32 - Gazingstock

> 32Partly, whilst **ye were made a gazingstock** both by reproaches and afflictions; and partly, whilst ye became companions of them that were so used.
>
> KJV

The Spiritual Activity Of The Male Power

Dan 8:6-7 – Ram Destroyed

> 6And he came to the ram that had two horns, which I had there seen standing before the river, **and ran unto him in the fury of his power.**
>
> 7And I saw him come close unto the ram, and he was moved with choler against him, and smote the ram, and brake his two horns: and there was no power in the ram to stand before him, but he cast him down to the ground, and stamped upon him: **and there was none that could deliver the ram out of his hand.**
>
> KJV

Rom 7:23 – Warlike Powers

23But I see another law in my members, *warring against the law of my mind*, and *bringing me into captivity* to the law of sin which is in my members.

KJV

God's Eyes

1 John 2:27 – No Man Need Teach You

27But *the anointing which ye have received of him abideth in you*, and ye need not that any man teach you: but as the same anointing teacheth you of all things, and is truth, and is no lie, and even as it hath taught you, *ye shall abide in him.*

KJV

Footnote # 28

28 **Idolatrous sacrifice**

The holy male calf (mind) is the only sacrifice acceptable to a pagan god.

Sacrifice to a pagan god is an act of spiritual adultery.

The death of the holy male calf (mind) divorces the body from Jehovah.

Idolatrous sacrifice kills the female Adam residing within the body.

The female power marries the widowed female Adam.

The female Adam and the body die spiritually after the female power marries them.

Deut 32:17 - Sacrifices

17 ***They sacrificed unto devils***, not to God; to gods whom they knew not, to new gods that came newly up, whom your fathers feared not.

KJV

Footnote # 29

29 **Covering**

The Hebrew word translated ***molten, Strong's #4541***, is spelled with the same Hebrew letters (in the same sequence) as the previous word in the Hebrew Lexicon, ***Strong's #4540***, which is rendered, ***covering,*** or ***outward adornment.*** Only the vowels are different.

Footnote # 30

30 **Basphemous Words**

Words reveal the nature and mind of the person speaking them.

Ps 73:6-9 – Words Of Pride

6Therefore pride compasseth them about as a chain; violence covereth them as a garment.

7Their eyes stand out with fatness: they have more than heart could wish.

8They are corrupt, and speak wickedly concerning oppression: they speak loftily.

9They set their mouth against the heavens, and their tongue walketh through the earth.

KJV

Footnote # 31

31 **False Gods**

"The male and female principalities that ride on the male calf (mind) (Note 22) of the mixed multitude(Note 6) are your gods."

a.
Individual Sin

Isa 42:20 - Blind To Sin

20Seeing many things, but *thou observest not; opening the ears, but he heareth not.*

KJV

2 Cor 4:4 – Blinded Minds

4In whom *the god of this world hath blinded the minds of them which believe not,* lest the light of the glorious gospel of Christ, who is the image of God, should shine unto them.

KJV

1 John 2:11 – Blinded Eyes

11But he that hateth his brother is in darkness, and walketh in darkness, and knoweth not whither he goeth, because that *darkness hath blinded his eyes*.

KJV

b.

The King's Sin

1 Kings 12:26-29 - Jeroboam

26And Jeroboam said in his heart, Now shall the kingdom return to the house of David:

27If this people go up to do sacrifice in the house of the LORD at Jerusalem, then shall the heart of this people turn again unto their lord, even unto Rehoboam king of Judah, and they shall kill me, and go again to Rehoboam king of Judah.

28Whereupon the king took counsel, and made two calves of gold, and said unto them, It is too much for you to go up to Jerusalem: behold thy gods, O Israel, which brought thee up out of the land of Egypt.

29And *he set the one [calf] in Bethel, and the other[calf] put he in Dan*.

KJV

Footnote # 32

32 **The Wickedness Of Man**

Humanity are the descendants of the female Adam who committed adultery with the Serpent.

Everyone born of a woman inherits the Serpent's nature.

Prov 22:15 – Foolish Youth

15*Foolishness* is bound in the heart of a child; but the rod of correction shall drive it far from him.

KJV

Gen 6:5 – Wicked Maturity

5And GOD saw that the wickedness of man was great in the earth, and that every imagination of ***the thoughts of his heart was only evil continually.***

KJV

1 Cor 4:5 – Spiritual Darkness

5Therefore judge nothing before the time, until the Lord come, who both will bring to light ***the hidden things of darkness***, and will make manifest the counsels of the hearts: and then shall every man have praise of God.

KJV

2 Cor 4:2 – Dishonesty

2But have renounced the ***hidden things of dishonesty***, not walking in craftiness, nor handling the word of God deceitfully; but by manifestation of the truth commending ourselves to every man's conscience in the sight of God.

KJV

Footnote # 33

33 **Cruelty In Israel**

Israel is a chameleon.

When he is attached to Jehovah, he is righteous.

When he is separated from Jehovah, he is cruel.

Lam 4:3 – Cruel As The Ostrich

> ³Even the sea monsters draw out the breast, they give suck to their young ones: the daughter of ***my people is become cruel***, like the ostriches in the wilderness.
>
> KJV

(See, also, Note 32)

Footnote # 34

34 **Personality**

The emotional and intellectual aspects of the body.

Footnote # 35

35 **Ox**

The body, including its emotional and intellectual aspects.

Humanity without the soul of God.

Job 40:15 - Behemoth

15Behold now behemoth, which I made with thee; *he eateth grass as an ox.*

KJV

Footnote # 36

36 **Immortality**

All Israel shall attain immortality in the world to come.

Isa 11:11-12 – A Second Time

11And it shall come to pass in that day, that the Lord shall set ***his hand again the second time to recover the remnant of his people***, which shall be left, from Assyria, and from Egypt, and from Pathros, and from Cush, and from Elam, and from Shinar, and from Hamath, and from the islands of the sea.

12And he shall set up an ensign for the nations, and ***shall assemble the outcasts of Israel, and gather together the dispersed of Judah from the four corners of the earth***.

KJV

Rom 11:26 – All Israel Saved

26And so ***all Israel shall be saved***: as it is written, There shall come out of Sion the Deliverer, and shall turn away ungodliness from Jacob:

KJV

(See, Also, Note 40.)

Footnote # 37

37 The Enforcer

Satan is the enforcer of Jehovah's righteous Sowing & Reaping Judgment.

Ps 17:13 – The Lash

13 Arise, O Lord, disappoint him, cast him down: deliver my soul from **the wicked, which is thy sword**:

KJV

In that capacity, on a personal level, Satan is the Accuser of the Brethren.

Job 1:9-11 – On Trial

9 Then Satan answered the Lord, and said, Doth Job fear God for nought?

10 Hast not thou made an hedge about him, and about his house, and about all that he hath on every side? thou hast blessed the work of his hands, and his substance is increased in the land.

11 But put forth thine hand now, and touch all that he hath, and he will curse thee to thy face.

KJV

(See, also, Note 44.)

Footnote # 38

38 Idolatrous Communication

Communication such as **speaking to**, or **hearing from**, spiritual entities, is the worship of false gods, which is idolatry.

Ezek 23:37 - Idolatry

> **37**That they have committed adultery, and blood is in their hands, and **with their idols have they committed adultery**, and have also caused their sons, whom they bare unto me, to pass for them through the fire, to devour them.

KJV

Footnote # 39

39 **Abraham's Seed**

Abraham's seed is righteous Adam in the earth of humanity.

Gal 3:16 – One Seed

16Now to Abraham and his seed were the promises made. He saith not, And to seeds, as of many; but as of one, ***And to thy seed, which is Christ***.

KJV

Adam is one immortal soul that is increasing into many points of light in the heaven, and many earthen bodies in the earth of Asiyah, the Universe of Action.

Gen 15:5 – Seed As The Stars

5And he brought him forth abroad, and said, Look now toward heaven, and tell the stars, if thou be able to number them: and he said unto him, ***So shall thy seed be***.

KJV

Gen 28:14-15 – Seed As The Dust

14And ***thy seed shall be as the dust of the earth***, and thou shalt spread abroad to the west, and to the east, and to the north, and to the south: and in thee and in thy seed shall all the families of the earth be blessed.

15And, behold, I am with thee, and will keep thee in all places whither thou goest, and will bring thee again into this land; for I will not leave thee, until I have done that which I have spoken to thee of.

    KJV

(See, also, Note 41.)

Footnote # 40

40 Righteous Adam, Jehovah's Son, shall join with Abraham's seed, the female Adam in the earth of humanity, and she shall give birth to a Son:

Isa 9:6-7 – A Son

6For unto us a child is born, unto us a son is given: and the government shall be upon his shoulder: and his name shall be called Wonderful, Counsellor, The mighty God, The everlasting Father, The Prince of Peace.

7Of the increase of his government and peace there shall be no end, upon the throne of David, and upon his kingdom, to order it, and to establish it with judgment and with justice from henceforth even for ever. The zeal of the Lord of hosts will perform this.

KJV

And the Son that the female Adam gives birth to shall be a husband and a savior to the physical body that he dwells in:

Isa 62:4-5 - Married

4Thou shalt no more be termed Forsaken; neither shall thy land any more be termed Desolate: but thou shalt be called Hephzi-bah, and thy land Beulah: for the LORD delighteth in thee, and **thy land shall be married**.

5For as a young man marrieth a virgin, **so shall thy sons marry thee:** and as the bridegroom rejoiceth over the bride, so shall thy God rejoice over thee.

KJV

(See, also, Note 39**Error! Bookmark not defined.**.)

Eph 5:23 – Husband & Saviour

23For the husband is the head of the wife, even as Christ is the head of the church: and he is the saviour of the body.

KJV

Footnote # 41

41 A Spiritual Body

Adam's soul shall be given a different, incorruptible form.

The physical body as well as the soul shall be resurrected, and the sparks of the female Adam, Abraham's seed, shall be clothed with spiritual bodies.

Nachmanides

> "It has thus been explained that the World to Come is not the World of Souls but an enduring world created for the people [to be] **resurrected in body and soul**.
>
> "The existence of the [human] soul when it is united with **a knowledge of the most high** is comparable to the existence of angels, which is made possible by [that comprehension].
>
> "The ascendancy of the soul over the [physical] body annuls the physical powers [of the body], as we have previously mentioned, and causes **the [physical] body to exist without food and drink** just as the soul exists and as Moses was sustained on Mount [Sinai] for 40 days." (Rambam, The Gate of Reward, Shilo Publishing House, Inc. 1983, pp 109-110.) (Emphasis added.)

(See, Also, Note 36.)

1 Cor 15:44-45 – A Spiritual Body

> **44** It is sown a natural body; it is raised a spiritual body. There is a natural body, and there is a spiritual body.

45 And so it is written, The first man Adam was made a living soul; the last Adam was made a quickening spirit.

KJV

Footnote # 42

42 **Sowing & Reaping**

The Sowing & Reaping Judgment is the expression of Jehovah's Anger . . .

Hos 10:12-13 – Mercy Or Iniquity

12*Sow to yourselves in righteousness, reap in mercy*; break up your fallow ground: for it is time to seek the Lord, till he come and rain righteousness upon you.

13*Ye have plowed wickedness, ye have reaped iniquity*; ye have eaten the fruit of lies: because thou didst trust in thy way, in the multitude of thy mighty men.

KJV

. . . and Satan is the enforcer of the Sowing & Reaping Judgment.

Job 1:12 – In Satan's Power

12And the LORD said unto Satan, **Behold, all that he hath is in thy power**; only upon himself put not forth thine hand. So Satan went forth from the presence of the LORD .

KJV

Hos 8:7 - Wind & Whirlwind

7For they have sown the wind, and **they shall reap the whirlwind**: it hath no stalk: the bud shall yield no meal: if so be it yield, the strangers shall swallow it up.

KJV

Gal 6:7 – Sowing & Reaping

7Be not deceived; God is not mocked: for ***whatsoever a man soweth, that shall he also reap.***

KJV

(See, also, Note 44.)

Footnote # 43

43 Satan Turned Back

Jehovah's mercy opposes his own righteous Sowing & Reaping Judgment.

Heb 12:1 – Easily Beset

> **1**Wherefore seeing we also are compassed about with so great a cloud of witnesses, let us lay aside every weight, and **the sin which doth so easily beset us**, and let us run with patience the race that is set before us,
>
> KJV

Zech 3:2 – Satan Rebuked

> **2**And the Lord said unto Satan, **The Lord rebuke thee, O Satan**; even the Lord that hath chosen Jerusalem rebuke thee: is not this a brand plucked out of the fire?
>
> KJV

Acts 5:31 - Repentance

> **31**Him hath God exalted with his right hand to be a Prince and a Saviour, for **to give repentance to Israel, and forgiveness of sins**.
>
> KJV

Footnote # 44

44 **Good Or Evil**

Jehovah gives us a choice:

We either learn from his instruction, or we experience the consequences of our behavior:

Deut 30:15-18 – Life & Good

15See, I have set before thee this day **life and good**, and **death and evil**;

16In that I command thee this day to love the Lord thy God, to walk in his ways, and to **keep his commandments** and his statutes and his judgments, **that thou mayest live and multiply**: and the Lord thy God shall bless thee in the land whither thou goest to possess it.

17But if thine heart turn away, so that **thou wilt not hear**, but shalt be drawn away, and worship other gods, and serve them;

18I denounce unto you this day, that **ye shall surely perish**, and that ye shall not prolong your days upon the land, whither thou passest over Jordan to go to possess it.

KJV

(See, also, Note 42.)

Footnote # 45

45 Heart Center

Jehovah gave Moses two additional spiritual regions from the world to come.

Righteous Adam is the world to come.

The **heart** and **mind** of the world to come were now inside of Moses.

Righteous Adam would be Moses' constant companion from that point in time.

1 Sam 10:9 – Another Heart

> **9**And it was so, that when he had turned his back to go from Samuel, **God gave him another heart**: and all those signs came to pass that day.
>
> KJV

Phil 2:5 – Another Mind

> **5**Let this mind be in you, which was also in Christ Jesus:
>
> KJV

Moses received the help that Jehovah promised the female Adam.

Gen 2:18 – Help Meet

> **18**And the Lord God said, It is not good that the man should be alone; **I will make him an help meet for him**.
>
> KJV

Footnote # 46

46 **Another Country**

A Neshamah that is permanently joined to a body, ***rolls out*** a material environment for itself, which manifests itself as the elements of the lifestyle that it reflects in the physical world.

The Neshamah level of consciousness, or mind, is so alien to the thought process of the body, that the personality experiencing it can be likened to ***a citizen of another country***.

Phil 3:20 - Heavenly Citizenship

> **20*But our citizenship is in heaven***. And we eagerly await a Savior from there, the Lord Jesus Christ,
>
> NIV

Footnote # 47

47 Neshamah

There are five grades of soul:

Nefesh – the life of the body that is in the blood

Ruach – intellectual spirit

Neshamah – the spiritual, intellectual soul

Chayah – the life force of the immortal world

Yechida – soul unity with God

A Neshamah that is permanently joined to a body **rolls out** an environment for itself, which manifests itself, spiritually, as a level of consciousness called **mind**.

The Neshamah grade of soul is called **the spiritual, intellectual soul that comes from God**, or **the Mind of God**.

In the New Testament, the Neshamah is called **the Mind of Christ**.

Moses received a **Neshamah**, the spiritual, intellectual soul that comes from God.

Soncino Zohar, Bereshith, Section 1 Page 62a

> The **neshamah (spiritual soul)** emerges and enters between the gorges of the mountains, where it is joined by the ruah (intellectual spirit).
>
> It descends then below where the nefesh (vital spirit) joins the ruah, and all three form a unity.'
>
> R. Judah said: 'The nefesh and the ruah are intertwined together, whereas **the neshamah resides in a man's character-an abode which cannot be discovered or located.**

Should a man strive towards purity of life, ***he is aided*** thereto ***by a holy neshamah***, whereby he is purified and sanctified and attains the title of "saint".

Footnote # 48

48 The Will Of God

The Will of God manifested as the spiritual government of Righteous Adam,(Note 13) **dries up** the waters of Satan's emotional sea, and imparts the life of Righteous Adam's **dry land** to the human soul that is separated from God

Isa 9:6-7 – Government Of God

> **6**For unto us a child is born, unto us a son is given: **and the government shall be upon his shoulder**: and his name shall be called Wonderful, Counsellor, The mighty God, The everlasting Father, The Prince of Peace.
>
> **7**Of **the increase of his government and peace there shall be no end**, upon the throne of David, and upon his kingdom, to order it, and to establish it with judgment and with justice from henceforth even forever. The zeal of the Lord of hosts will perform this.
>
> KJV

Gen 1:9 – Dry Land

> **9**And God said, Let the waters under the heaven be gathered together unto one place, **and let the dry land appear:** and it was so.
>
> KJV

2 Kings 2:8 – Waters Divided

> **8**And Elijah took his mantle, and wrapped it together, and smote the waters, and **they were**

divided hither and thither, so that ***they two went over on dry ground***.

KJV

2 Kings 2:14 – Waters Parted

14And he took the mantle of Elijah that fell from him, and smote the waters, and said, Where is the Lord God of Elijah? and when he also had smitten ***the waters, they parted*** hither and thither: ***and Elisha went over***.

KJV

Acts 1:8 – Power Of God

8***But ye shall receive power, after that the Holy Ghost is come upon you***: and ye shall be witnesses unto me both in Jerusalem, and in all Judaea, and in Samaria, and unto the uttermost part of the earth.

KJV

Footnote # 49

49 Witnesses

The Neshamah is the male mind of God.

The seed of a Neshamah can be given to another person, when Righteous Adam permits it.

The seed is a thought that comes from the Word of God.

The male seed of Righteous Adam is manifested in the earth as the esoteric understanding of the Word of God

A desire for righteousness below, attracts the heavenly forces that send forth the Neshamah.

Ezek 9:4 – The Mind of God

> **4**And the Lord said unto him, Go through the midst of the city, through the midst of Jerusalem, and set ***a mark upon the foreheads*** of the men that sigh and that cry for all the abominations that be done in the midst thereof.
>
> KJV

John 5:36 – God-Motivated Behavior

> **36**But I have greater witness than that of John: for the works which the Father hath given me to finish, the same works that I do, bear ***witness of me, that the Father hath sent me***.
>
> KJV

Footnote # 50

50 **Elohim, The Judge**

Elohim literally means *God,* or *judge.*

It is the name of the creator in Genesis, Chapter 1.

It is also used to describe the presence of God in a man.

Footnote # 51

51 **Moses & Joshua**

Joshua, the Ephraimite, and Moses, had a teacher-disciple intimacy, and Miriam and Aaron were jealous.

(See, also, Note 12.)

Footnote # 52

52 Abel Lives

a.

Joshua in verse 17, and the Eternal One speaking through Moses in verse 18, are the two witnesses required by law to execute judgment for sin in the camp.

b.

Abel died to the heavenly world, but he did not cease to exist.

He continues on under the ground of Cain's world, where the Serpent's agents enforce the Law of Jehovah's Righteous Sowing & Reaping Judgment, without mercy.

Gen 4:8 – Abel Slain

> **8**And Cain talked with Abel his brother: and it came to pass, when they were in the field, that ***Cain rose up against Abel his brother, and slew him***.
>
> KJV

Gen 4:10 – Abel's Blood

> **10**And he said, What hast thou done? the voice of ***thy brother's blood crieth unto me from the ground***.
>
> KJV

Heb 11:4 – Abel's Sacrifice

4By faith Abel offered unto God a more excellent sacrifice than Cain, by which he obtained witness that he was righteous, God testifying of his gifts: and by *it he being dead yet speaketh.*

KJV

Luke 1:67 – The Soul Of Abel In Men

67And his father Zacharias was filled with the Holy Ghost, and *prophesied, saying,*

KJV

(See, also, Note 69.)

Footnote # 53

53 **Cain's Control**

Cain is a serpent like his father.

Cain controls Abel with continuous stinging bites to his neck.

Prov 23:32 – A Serpent's Bite

32At the last it **biteth like a serpent**, and stingeth like an adder.

KJV

Acts 7:54 – Bitten

54When they heard these things, they were cut to the heart, and **they gnashed on him with their teeth**.

KJV

(See, also, verses 5b, 20.)

Footnote # 54

54 **Lord *and* Master**

Adon is a masculine noun which means ***lord*** or ***master***. The most frequent use of the word is a ***human lord***, but it is also used of divinity.

When used of humans, ***Adon*** refers to authority over slaves, people, a wife or a household.

Aaron addressed Moses as ***lord*** to acknowledge his authority to bring destructive judgment upon the people.

Footnote # 55

55 **Evil Sons**

Aaron and Moses knew that the people had **an evil inclination.**

(See, also, Note 54)

The revealed purpose of man is to distinguish the light (nature) of God within his border, from the light of God that surrounds him.

The sons of God are called **morning stars** because they distinguish the light within themselves from the surrounding light of God, their source.

Dan 12:3 - Brightness

> ³And they that be wise shall **shine as the brightness of the firmament**; and they that turn many to righteousness as the stars for ever and ever.
>
> KJV

The sons of God lament, however, when Jehovah corrects their evil side.

Job 38:7 – Morning Stars

> ⁷The sons of God cry out with joy when they are united [with God], but **they become evil [when their thoughts separate them from him]**.
>
> ATB

The Hebrew word translated **to shout**, can also be translated **to mourn, or wail,**

Rom 6:6 – Body Of Sin

6Knowing this, that our old man is crucified with him, ***that the body of sin might be destroyed***, that henceforth we should not serve sin.

KJV

Col 3:9 – Old Man

9Lie not one to another, seeing that ye have ***put off the old man with his deeds***;

KJV

(See, also, Note 33.)

Footnote # 56

56 Spiritual Circumcision

Circumcise yourself!

Cut off Cain, the foreskin of the unholy male calf that joins you to the female power.

Footnote # 57

57 Idolatry & The Serpent

Idolatry in Israel strengthens the Serpent.

Soncino Zohar, Bereshith, Section 1, Page 171a

. . . [A]s the upholders of the Torah become weaker, strength is thereby gained by him who has no legs to stand upon. For when God said to the serpent, "upon thy belly shalt thou go" (Gen. III, 14), the serpent had his supports and legs cut off so that he was left with nothing to stand on. But **when Israel neglect to support the Torah, they thereby provide him with supports and legs on which to stand firm and upright.**

Footnote # 58

58 **Naked**

The people were loosed from Jehovah, their spiritual cover.

Gen 3:7 – Eyes Opened

7And the eyes of them both were opened, ***and they knew that they were naked***; and they sewed fig leaves together, ***and made themselves aprons.***

KJV

Footnote # 59

59 **Separated From God**

The Torah (Word of God) ***is symbolized by water.***

Soncino Zohar, Bereshith, Section 1, Page 12b

> .... *[T]he Torah, which is symbolised by water*, possesses the virtue of implanting in her devotees a mobile soul derived *from the place called "living"* (hayah) ....

The letters of the Torah are the male seed, **which contains the hidden, esoteric wisdom.** ...

Soncino Zohar, Shemoth, Section 2, Page

> ... [T]he **words of the Torah have also an** ***esoteric significance***, and ***every word therein contains hidden seeds of wisdom***, comprehensible only to the wise who are familiar with the ways of the Torah.

... which fall upon the Shekinah below to complete her male aspect.

The people were bound to Jehovah through Aaron's spiritual semen, which consists of water (Spirit of God) and seed (Word of God).

The female power had to withdraw Aaron's male seed, that is, his doctrine, from the people, before she separated them from Jehovah and formed her male calf (mind) in them.

This means that the people must have rejected what Aaron taught them, and believed the Serpent's doctrine.

What is the Serpent's doctrine?

Gen 3:5 – Like God

5For God doth know that in the day ye eat thereof, then your eyes shall be opened, and *ye shall be as gods, knowing good and evil.*

KJV

How does the Serpent teach his doctrine?

Through human beings who host his mind.

(See, also, Notes 25, 62.)

Footnote # 60

60 Ye Are Gods

Eternal life is a potential reality for human beings who are imbued with a soul that comes from God.

Israel has a soul that comes from God, but they die like human beings because of the evil inclination, the fallen nature that they inherited from Adam, and because of **the sin of the golden calf**.

Ps 82:6-7 – Ye Shall Die Like Men

6I have said, ***Ye are gods***; and all of you are children of the most High.

7But ***ye shall die like men***, and fall like one of the princes.

KJV

Footnote # 61

61 Unholy Male Calf

Struggle For Spiritual Power

The mixed multitude(Note 6) ***desired spiritual power***, so they married Abel, the royal seed of the Shekinah,(Note 10) to the female power,(Notes 23. 28) who formed **an unholy, male calf** (mind)(Note 22) in the people...

Gen 37:28 – Joseph Sold

> **28**Then there passed by Midianites merchantmen; and they drew and lifted up Joseph out of the pit, ***and sold Joseph to the Ishmeelites for twenty pieces of silver***: and they brought Joseph into Egypt.
>
> KJV

. . . which ultimately led their descendants into bondage in Egypt.

Ex 2:23 - Slavery

> 23 And it came to pass in process of time, that the king of Egypt died: and ***the children of Israel sighed by reason of the bondage***, and they cried, and their cry came up unto God by reason of the bondage.
>
> KJV

Judgment For Illegal Spiritual Power

Sin is a departure from Godliness, that is revealed in the personality.

Ps 68:31 – Rod Of Correction

31Correct the people [who have the waters of] life with the rod, [because the female power(Note 28) has married] the [female] calves [that the Shekinah produced, and] assembled **the mighty bulls [of Bashan]**.

ATB

The reality of forgiveness is a change of nature, and a change of the circumstances of this life.

Hos 14:2-3 – Sin No More

2Lay hold of the mind that Jehovah listens to, and say to him, "complete the good [Adam within me by] assembling the [holy male] calf at the edge(Note 22) [of the earth, so that Righteous Adam] might [come into existence, and] take away [our] guilt,"

3Asshur shall not save us; we will not ride upon horses: **neither will we say any more to the work of our hands, Ye are our gods**: for in thee the fatherless findeth mercy.

KJV

All judgment is towards the sin nature.

The purpose of God's judgment to to weaken the sin nature, so that Righteous Adam stands up in power and defeats the enemies of our soul.

The judgment upon the male calf (mind) is to break its neck, which forces the withdrawal of the unholy male seed from the male aspect of the Shekinah below.

We are talking about a mind.

The unholy male calf is the Carnal Mind.

The holy male calf is the Mind of Christ.

Soncino Zohar, Shemoth, Raya Mehemna 43a

> AND EVERY FIRSTLING OF AN ASS THOU SHALT REDEEM WITH A LAMB, AND IF THOU WILT NOT REDEEM IT... ***THOU SHALT BREAK HIS NECK.***
>
> ***The ass and the lamb symbolize the evil and the good inclinations.*** The very evil can be turned into good by repentance: the "ass" ***must be redeemed by a "lamb"***.
>
> In other words, ***even if a man is an "ass", a spiritual ignoramus, he can be redeemed from the exile of darkness*** and be included in the redemption of Israel, "the scattered sheep" (Jer. L, 17).
>
> But if he does not repent, "***thou shalt break his neck,***"

(See, also, Notes 25, 59.)

> meaning, he belongs to ***the stiffnecked ones who will be blotted out from the Book of Life***,
>
> For concerning such unrepentant sinners it is written: "***Whosoever hath sinned against me, him will I blot out of my book***" (Ex. XXII, 33).

The spiritual reality of the calf's broken neck, is ***that the unholy male seed withdraws from the female calf***, (mind) and Christ Jesus, the Lamb of God, marries her.

We are talking about the mind of a human being.

The spiritual reality of judgment upon the unholy male calf (mind) is that the Carnal Mind is broken up and destroyed, and the Mind of Christ becomes the ruling mind of the person having this experience.

John 1:29 – Lamb Of God

11The next day John seeth Jesus coming unto him, and saith, **Behold the Lamb of God**, which taketh away the sin of the world.

KJV

The Lord Jesus Christ burns the unholy male calf (mind) in the Lake of Fire.

The Lake of Fire is the Mind of Christ.

The fire that destroys the Carnal Mind is the esoteric doctrine of the Word of God. The very sound of it breaks the rocks of the Carnal Mind asunder.

Jer 20:9 – Fire In My Bones

9Then I said, I will not make mention of him, nor speak any more in his name. But his word was in mine heart as a burning fire shut up in my bones, and I was weary with forbearing, and I could not stay.

KJV

Rev 17:16 – Burnt With Fire

16And the ten horns which thou sawest upon the beast, these shall hate the whore, and shall make her desolate and naked, and shall eat her flesh, and **burn her with fire**.

KJV

Reiteration

16The ten powers (Sefirot) of the Beast that you saw [revealed through the fallen nature of man] shall hate the whore, [the repentant, female Adam, who is now the Bride of Christ], and shall [seek] to destroy [her male offspring], and strip him of [the protection of his father, the Lord Jesus Christ, but the Lord Jesus] **shall burn [the Beast in the Lake of] Fire**, and consume its flesh . . . .

    ATB

. . . to force the male seed of the female power to withdraw.. . . .

which restores the spiritual virginity of the man . . . .

Rev 14:4 - Virgins

4 These are they which were not defiled with women; *for they are virgins*. These are they which follow the Lamb whithersoever he goeth. These were redeemed from among men, being the firstfruits unto God and to the Lamb.

    KJV

. . . and Christ Jesus marries the female calf (mind) within the individual.

Rom 5:11 – The Atonement

11And not only so, but we also joy in God through our Lord Jesus Christ, by whom *we have now received the atonement*.

    KJV

(See, also, Note 22.)

Footnote # 62

62 Blotted Out

The day is coming, when all the thoughts of a man's heart will be judged.

Dan 7:10 – Judgment Day

10A fiery stream issued and came forth from before him: thousand thousands ministered unto him, and ten thousand times ten thousand stood before him: ***the judgment was set***, and the books were opened.

KJV

Rev 20:12 – According To Their Works

12And I saw the dead, small and great, stand before God; and the books were opened: and another book was opened, which is ***the book of life: and the dead were judged out of those things which were written in the books, according to their works.***

KJV

Eternal life will be awarded . . .

Isa 25:8 - Death Swallowed Up

8***He will swallow up death in victory***; and the Lord God will wipe away tears from off all faces; and the rebuke of his people shall he take away from off all the earth: for the Lord hath spoken it.

KJV

1 Cor 15:55 – Sting Of Death

55O death, where is thy sting? O grave, where is thy victory?

KJV

. . . . but not to everyone.

Ex 32:33 – Sin Against Jehovah

33And the Lord said unto Moses, ***Whosoever hath sinned against me, him will I blot out of my book.***

KJV

Rom 6:23 – Wages Of Sin

23*For the wages of sin is death*; but the gift of God is eternal life through Jesus Christ our Lord.

KJV

(See, also, Notes 65, 66, 67.)

Footnote # 63

63 Book of Life

The names of the people who are to inherit eternal life are written in a spiritual book called **The Book of Life**. This book is locked up and sealed with many seals, and hidden away in a secret place.

Esoteric doctrine, understood with **the mind of God**, is the only key that unlocks **The Book of Life**, and only those whose names are written in the Book, believe the doctrine when they find it.

Ps 69:28 – In The Book

> **28**Let them be blotted out of the book of the living, and **not be written with the righteous**.
>
> KJV

What is the **Book of the Life**?

The Book of Life is the Book of Adam Kadmon, the Living One.

Adam Kadmon, primordial human, is the soul of the Torah (Word of God).

Soncino Zohar, Bemidbar, Section 3, Page 152a

> The Community of Israel is the body which receives *[Adam Kadmon], the soul [of the Torah], to wit, the "Glory of Israel";*

Sparks of the soul of Righteous Adam incarnate as the **additional Israelite soul**, and become the **Glory of Jehovah** within Israel, or **the Glory of Israel.**

Adam Kadmon, primordial human and the soul of the Torah (Word of God), is the soul of Righteous Adam.

Soncino Zohar, Bemidbar, Section 3, Page 152a

.... "and the super-soul is the Ancient Holy One."

The Book of Life is the Torah.

The name, or nature, that wrote, or engraved the Word of Gd, is the nature of the Living One, which is the nature of God himself.

Soncino Zohar, Shemoth, Section 2, Page 90b

.... [S]o is ***the whole Torah [Word of God] engraved in*** the Ten Words (Decalogue), and ***these Ten Words are the Name of the Holy One, and the whole Torah is thus one Name, the Holy Name of God Himself.***

Those who are ***written with the righteous***, are the spiritual children who are ***written upon, or engraved with,*** the nature of Righteous Adam.

(See, also, Notes 11, 13, 18, 14)

Soncino Zohar, Bereshith, Section 1, Page 1b

And who is it that upholds the world and causes the patriarchs to appear? ***It is the voice of tender children studying the Torah; and for their sakes the world is saved....'***

(See, also, vs 15-16.)

These ***spiritual children*** are Torah Scholars of any age.

They are the spiritual offspring of Righteous Adam, the Son of Adam Kadmon, the soul of the Torah (Word of God).

They are ***the words of the Word of God*** ....

Ps 12:6 – Pure Words

6The words of the Lord are pure words: as silver tried in a furnace of earth, purified seven times.
KJV

. . . . written in the earthen hearts of the scholars [who study] the Word of God . . . .

Prov 3:3 – Tables Of The Heart

3Let not mercy and truth forsake thee: bind them about thy neck; write them upon the table of thine heart:
   KJV

. . . . who have pierced through to ***the soul of the Word of God***.

These are they who will inherit eternal life.

The passport to eternal life is a spiritual experience called, ***piercing through to the soul of the Word of God***.

Eternal life is found in the esoteric doctrine of he Word of God!

Footnote # 64

64 **Moses Intercedes**

The two additional energy centers that Moses received in the mount imbued him with the full power and authority of the Government of God. This authority was revealed as ***Moses' male mind***.

(See, also, Note 48.)

Moses knew that Righteous Adam, his male mind, was stronger than the female power that had exalted itself through the mixed multitude.

Moses knew that he would not be widowed, or made a laughingstock, like Aaron was.

(See, also, Notes 11, 27.)

Moses was fully equipped to separate the people from the Evil Inclination.

(See, also, Notes 79, 69.)

Footnote # 65

65 Teach My People

Moses is instructed to prepare the people for the day that Jehovah will reveal the hidden motives of their heart:

Ps 44:20-21 – Secrets Of The Heart

20If we have forgotten the name of our God, or stretched out our hands to a strange god;

21Shall not God search this out? for **he knoweth the secrets of the heart.**

KJV

. . . to train them to distinguish between the thoughts of the animal mind and the thoughts of Christ.

Prov 2:9 - Understanding

9Then shalt **thou understand righteousness, and judgment, and equity; yea, every good path.**

KJV

Eph 4:11-12 – Righteousness

11And he gave some, apostles; and some, prophets; and some, evangelists; and some, pastors and teachers;

12For the perfecting of the saints, for the work of the ministry, for the edifying of the body of Christ:

KJV

Footnote # 66

66 Motives Judged

Jehovah knows all about the secret sins in the heart of fallen man. They cannot be hidden from him, and he has set a time to reveal and judge them.

Jer 17:10 – Heart & Reins

> **10**I the Lord search the heart, I try the reins, even **to give every man according to his ways, and according to the fruit of his doings.**
>
> KJV

(See, also, Notes 62, 65, 69.)

Rev 20:12 – Books Opened

> **12**And I saw the dead, small and great, stand before God; and **the books were opened**: and another book was opened, which is the book of life: and the dead were judged out of those things which were written in the books, according to their works.
>
> KJV

Footnote # 67

67 **Hidden Sins**

Jer 17:9 – Deceitful Heart

⁹*The heart is deceitful above all things, and desperately wicked*: who can know it?

KJV

1 Cor 4:5 - Hidden Darkness

⁵Therefore judge nothing before the time, until the Lord come, who both will bring to light ***the hidden things of darkness***, and will make manifest the counsels of the hearts: and then shall every man have praise of God

KJV

(See, also, Note 65, 69.)

Footnote # 68

67 Angel Of The Covenant

The Angel of the Covenant[Note 68] stays with Israel, even when they go into captivity.

(See, also, Note 79.)

Soncino Zohar, Bereshith, Section 1

"And Isaac dwelt by Beer-lahai-roi" (lit. the well of the living and seeing one), that is, as the Aramaic paraphrase has it, "the well where appeared ***the Angel of the Covenant***",[Note 68] ***to wit, the Shekinah, to which Isaac became attached***, thereby drawing upon himself the blessing of the Almighty.'

Ex 23:20-21 – Protective Angel

20Behold, ***I send an Angel before thee***, to keep thee in the way, and to bring thee into the place which I have prepared.

21Beware of him, and obey his voice, provoke him not; for ***he will not pardon your transgressions***: for my name is in him.

KJV

. . . . He will not pardon you, unless you repent.

The Angel of the Covenant is also called **the Shekinah in captivity**, or, **the Shekinah below**.

Footnote # 69

68 **Sins Covered**

Forgiveness of sin is a process:

1. Conviction – The person must be convinced that what they did is a sin.

2. Confession – The person must confess that they committed the specific sin that has been revealed.

3. Repentance – The ability to experience a godly sorrow is granted.

4. Forgiveness – Jehovah protects the person from his own righteous, Sowing & Reaping Judgment, which is enforced by Satan.

Jehovah reveals sin and judges it, i.e., pronounces the personality guilty of that sin, for the specific purpose of forgiving that sin.

Ex 23:22 – An Enemy To Your Enemies

> **22**But if thou shalt indeed obey his voice, and do all that I speak; then *I will be an enemy unto thine enemies*, and an adversary unto thine adversaries.
>
> KJV

(See, also, 52, 66, 67.)

Eph 1:7 – Sins Forgiven

> **7**In whom we have redemption through his blood, the *forgiveness of sins*, according to the riches of his grace;
>
> KJV

Footnote # 70

70 **Struggle For Power**

Aaron was married to the Shekinah, his spiritual covering, who made the male calf (mind) that provided Aaron with ***the spiritual power*** to rescue the people from the idolatrous male nature that had married them.

(See, also, Notes 6, 8, 12, 74)

But, the mixed multitude chose the principality of the other side, which widowed Aaron, married the people who were Aaron's spiritual wife, and illegally acquired an unholy male calf (mind).

(See, also, Notes 6, 8, 12, 61.)

Footnote # 71

71 Swinging Door

A spiritual door, or window, separates the upper and the lower worlds.

Angels guard the side of the door that opens into the garden of Eden, and the serpent crouches at the side that opens into the lower world.

Gen 4:7 - Sin Behind The Door

> **7** If thou doest well, shalt thou not be accepted? and if thou doest not well, **sin lieth at the door**. And unto thee shall be his desire, and thou shalt rule over him.
>
> KJV

Footnote # 72

72 Adultery & Thigh

Adultery – Verse 26

The Hebrew word translated **unto me**, Strong's 413, is used metaphorically to refer to sexual intercourse.

It is translated **adultery** in verse 26, above.

Spiritual adultery is an illegal spiritual or mental attachment. Both spirit and mind are usually involved.

The Levites, Jehovah's priestly tribe, were adulterously attached to Pharaoh, through the unholy calf-mind that the female power had birthed within them.

Thigh –Verse 27

The Hebrew word translated **side**, Strong's 413, is the same Hebrew word translated **[Jacob's] thigh** in Genesis 32.

It means **generative parts**.

The Levites committed spiritual adultery with the female power, and produced an illegitimate calf mind.

After that, the unholy calf mind killed the mind of God which Jehovah had formed in the Levites.

Footnote # 73

73 Spiritual Universe Of Mind

The mind is a spiritual universe and a doorway to other spiritual worlds.

Every spiritual world has a counterpart, or reflection, in the earth.

Spiritual worlds are experienced through meditation.

Num 13:17 – Spy Out The Land

17 And Moses sent them to spy out the land of Canaan, and said unto them, Get you up this way southward, and go up into the mountain:

KJV

Num 13:28-29 – Inhabitants Of The Land

28 Nevertheless the people be strong that dwell in the land, and the cities are walled, and very great: and moreover we saw the children of Anak there.

29 The Amalekites dwell in the land of the south: and the Hittites, and the Jebusites, and the Amorites, dwell in the mountains: and the Canaanites dwell by the sea, and by the coast of Jordan.

KJV

Footnote # 74

74 Illegal Spiritual Power

Chochmah of Binah is a source of spiritual power that flows both from God, and from the ***other side***.

1 Kings 3:28 - Justice

28And all Israel heard of the judgment which the king had judged; and they feared the king: for they saw that ***the wisdom of God was in him, to do judgment.***

KJV

Ezek 13:18 - Witchcraft

18And say, Thus saith the Lord God; Woe to the women that sew pillows to all armholes, and make kerchiefs upon the head of every stature to hunt souls! ***Will ye hunt the souls of my people***, and will ye save the souls alive that come unto you?

KJV

Acts 8:9 - Sorcery

9But there was a certain man, called Simon, which before time in the same city ***used sorcery, and bewitched the people*** of Samaria, giving out that himself was some great one:

KJV

Acts 8:19-20 – Money For Power

19Saying, *Give me also this power*, that on whomsoever I lay hands, he may receive the Holy Ghost.

20But Peter said unto him, **Thy money perish with thee**, because thou hast thought that the gift of God may be purchased with money.

KJV

Footnote # 75

75 **Walls**

Walls represent separation – something that needs to be removed.

Josh 6:20 – Naked

20So the people shouted when the priests blew with the trumpets: and it came to pass, when the people heard the sound of the trumpet, and the people shouted with a great shout, that ***the wall fell down flat***, so that the people went up into the city, every man straight before him, and they took the city.

KJV

Footnote # 76

76 Armies Of God

The troops of Jehovah are the bodies that the Shekinah, the wife of the male Adam, is married to.

Ex 12:41 – Hosts Of The Lord

41And it came to pass at the end of the four hundred and thirty years, even the selfsame day it came to pass, that ***all the hosts of the Lord went out from the land of Egypt***.

KJV

Footnote # 77

77 **Moses is Adam**

Adam is the spiritual man that stands behind the human body.

Song 2:9 – Behind The Wall

9My beloved is like a roe or a young hart: behold, he **standeth behind our wall**, he looketh forth at the windows, shewing himself through the lattice.
KJV

Soncino Zohar, Shemoth, Section 2, Page 238a

"And they brought the tabernacle unto Moses", **Moses being a synonym of Adam.** The Tabernacle is symbolic of all the members of the Body when suffused with a holy desire for the union of the male and female principles.

Footnote # 78

78 **Consuming Fire**

Ex 13:21 - Pillar Of Fire

The fire of God is spiritual fire:

> **21**And the Lord went before them by day in a pillar of a cloud, to lead them the way; and ***by night in a pillar of fire***, to give them light; to go by day and night:
>
> KJV

Ex 3:2 - Burning Bush

> **2**And the angel of the Lord appeared unto him in ***a flame of fire out of the midst of a bush***: and he looked, and, behold, the bush burned with fire, and the bush was not consumed.
>
> KJV

The fire of God consumes sin.

Deut 4:24 – Purifying Fire

> **24**For the Lord thy God is a consuming fire, even a jealous God.
>
> KJV

Footnote # 79

79 Separation

The Threshing floor crushes the grain and separates the wheat from the inedible chaff.

The wheat signifies **the Shekinah in captivity**.

The chaff signifies **the mixed multitude**, which joined with the female power to form the unholy calf mind.

(See, also, Notes 6, 11, 23.)

2 Sam 24:21-23 - Harvest

21And Araunah said, Wherefore is my lord the king come to his servant? And David said, ***To buy the threshing floor*** of thee, to build an altar unto the Lord, that the plague may be stayed from the people.

22And Araunah said unto David, Let my lord the king take and offer up what seemeth good unto him: behold, here be oxen for burnt sacrifice, and threshing instruments and other instruments of the oxen for wood.

23All these things did Araunah, as a king, give unto the king. And Araunah said unto the king, The Lord thy God accept thee.

KJV

Heb 4:12 – Soul From Spirit

12For the word of God is quick, and powerful, and sharper than any twoedged sword, piercing even to the dividing asunder of soul and spirit, and of the joints and marrow, and is a discerner of the thoughts and intents of the heart.

KJV

(See, also, verses 6 and 20.)

Footnote # 80

80 **Before His Son**

God gave his only begotten Son to be the ***male seed***, which would save the Woman from her sins,

. . . . but he gave the Shekinah, the ***female seed***, before he gave his Son:

Soncino Zohar, Shemoth, Section 2 Page 134b

. . . [T]he Lord of the House, whose love is always directed towards the Matrona, like a husband who loves his wife always. "Whose heart is willing": that is, His heart goes out to Her, and Her heart to Him. And although their mutual love is so great that they never separate, yet "ye shall take from Him My heave offering", meaning, **"ye should take the Shekinah to dwell with you".**

The Holy One, blessed be He, unlike a human husband,

Soncino Zohar, Shemoth, Section 2, Page 135a

who would protest violently should anyone take from him the wife whom he so dearly loves, is greatly pleased when the Shekinah, whom He so loves, is "taken" from the supernal sphere, the abode of Love, to dwell below in the midst of Israel.

Happy is the lot of Israel and happy that of all those who are worthy of this.

(See, also, Note 11.)

Footnote # 81

81 Spiritual Relatives

Sexual intimacy between close relatives is called ***incest***.

Incest between spiritual principles and in spiritual relationships is acceptable to God.

Incest between physical people is forbidden in the Scripture.

Gen 20:2 – Wife and Sister

²And ***Abraham said of Sarah his wife, She is my sister***: and Abimelech king of Gerar sent, and took Sarah.

KJV

Song 4:10 – Sister and Bride

¹⁰*How fair is thy love, my sister, my spouse*! how much better is thy love than wine! and the smell of thine ointments than all spices!

KJV

(See, also, Note 12.)

Footnote # 82

82 Living Water

The **Living Water**, or the **Water of Life**, is **the spiritual semen** of Ze'ir Anpin, the son of Adam Kadmon, primordial human.

The radiant light that flows out from Adam Kadmon is the source of Ze'ir Anpin's seed.

This seed is the Word of God.

(See, also, Notes 11, 14.)

Soncino Zohar, Bereshith, Section 1, Page 15b

1. . . . Bereshith is the name used so long as the house was uninhabited.

2. When, however, it was sown with seed to make it habitable, **it was called Elohim**, hidden and mysterious.

3. The Zohar was hidden and withdrawn so long as the building was within and yet to bring forth, and

4. The house was extended only so far as to find room for the holy seed.

5. Before it had conceived and had extended sufficiently to be habitable, it was not called Elohim, but all was still included in the term Bereshith.

6. After it had acquired the name of Elohim, it brought forth offspring from the seed that had been implanted in it.

Reiteration

1. ***The Beginning*** is the name used so long as the Shekinah (the female Adam), the household of the male Adam, is unmarried.

2. When, however, the Shekinah is sown with the male seed (the letters of the Word of God) to make the Shekinah an habitation for God, the male seed is called ***Elohim***, the name of the hidden mystery [called ***the sons of God***].

3. The Shekinah extends only so far as five of the six Sefirot of her male aspect (Yesod, Hod, Netzach, Gevurah and Chesed), so as to provide a place for the holy male seed to join itself to the lower world.

4. The radiant light which contains the male seed is hidden and withdrawn from sight, however, for so long as the Shekinah is lying down under Cain, the shell that covers her, and has not yet brought forth a male offspring.

5. Before the male seed extends the five Sefirot of the Shekinah's male aspect to the six Sefirot by which the Shekinah becomes pregnant with the male child that makes her sufficient to be an habitation for God, the male offspring [that Jehovah desires] is not yet called Elohim; [but the sparks of the male seed which are destined to incarnate as the sons of God], are still included in the term ***Bereshith***, ***the Beginning***.

6. Then, after the male calf of the Shekinah comes into existence, this ***Beginning*** acquires the name ***Elohim*** and brings forth offspring [in the earth of humanity] from the male seed which was implanted in her; [and these offspring are called ***the sons of God***].

(See, also, Note 16.)

Moses:

Ex 2:10

10And the child grew, and she brought him unto Pharaoh's daughter, and he became her son. **And she called his name Moses: and she said, Because I drew him out of the water**.

KJV

Reference

Footnotes

Table Of Notes

Sorted By Note Number

Title	#	Comments
Idolatry For Leaders	1	
Emotional And Spiritual Weakness	2	
Spiritual Waters	3	
Stand up in God's power	4	
A Cart For Elohim	5	
Mixed Multitude	6	
Circular Universe	7	
Spiritual Wives	8	
Military Power of Jehovah	9	
Royal Female Seed	10	
Shekinah	11	
Spiritual Marriage	12	
Righteous Adam	13	
Well of Existence	14	
Manna Is Spiritual Food	15	
Manna, The Flesh Of The Shekinah	16	
The Neck Of Righteous Adam	17	
Engraving Tool	18	
Formed From The Dust	19	
End Of The Transgression	20	
Spiritual Altar	21	
Male Calf	22	
Female Power	23	
Grass	24	
Bonded To Jehovah	25	
Spiritual Arrogance	26	
Cuckold	27	
Idolatrous sacrifice	28	

Covering	29
Blasphemous Words	30
False gods	31
The Wickedness Of Man	32
Cruelty In Israel	33
Personality	34
Ox	35
Immortality	36
Enforcer	37
Idolatrous Communication	38
Abraham's Seed	39
A Physical Body	40
A Spiritual Body	41
Sowing & Reaping	42
Satan Turned Back	43
Good & Evil	44
Heart Center	45
Neshamah	47
Will Of God	48
Witnesses	49
Elohim, The Judge	50
Another Country	46
Moses & Joshua	51
Abel Lives	52
Cain's Control	53
Lord & Master	54
Evil Sons	55
Spiritual Circumcision	56
Idolatry & The Serpent	57
Naked	58
Separated From God	59
Ye Are Gods	60
Unholy Male Calf	61
Blotted Out	62
Book Of Life	63
Moses Intercedes	64
Teach My People	65
Motives Judged	66
Hidden Sins	67
Angel Of The Covenant	68
Sins Covered	69
Struggle For Power	70
Swinging Door	71
Adultery & Thigh	72

Spiritual Universe Of Mind	73	
Illegal Spiritual Power	74	
Walls	75	
Armies Of God	76	
Moses Is Adam	77	
Consuming Fire	78	
Separation	79	
Before The Son	80	
Spiritual Relatives	81	
Living Water	82	

Sorted By Scripture

(Old Testament Bolded)

Scripture	Key Phrase	Note #
1 Cor 1:21	Foolishness of Preaching	16
1 Cor 10:2-4	In The Cloud	8
1 Cor 15:34	Awake To Righteousness	6
1 Cor 15:4	Third Day	24
1 Cor 15:44-45	A Spiritual Body	41
1 Cor 15:55	Sting Of Death	62
1 Cor 4:5	Spiritual Darkness	32
1 Cor 4:5	Hidden Darkness	67
1 John 2:11	Blinded Eyes	31a
1 John 2:2	The Sins Of The World	22
1 John 2:27	No Man Need Teach You	27
1 Kings 12:26-29	Jeroboam	31b
1 Kings 19:13	God's Power	4
1 Kings 3:28	Justice	74
1 Sam 10:9	Another Heart	45
1 Tim 2:5	Only One Mediator	11
2 Cor 10:4	Spiritual Weapons	9
2 Cor 4:2	Dishonesty	32
2 Cor 4:4	Blinded Minds	31a
2 Kings 18:4	Idolatry In Israel	2
2 Kings 2:14	Waters Parted	48
2 Kings 2:8	Waters Divided	48
2 Sam 1:26	Passing The Love Of Women	12
2 Sam 12:9-10	Uriah	16
2 Sam 24:21-23	Harvest	79
Acts 1:8	Power Of God	48
Acts 13:8	Elymas	26
Acts 5:31	Repentance	43
Acts 7:54	Bitten	53
Acts 8:19-20	Money For Power	74
Acts 8:9	Sorcery	74
Col 2:10	Complete	25
Col 3:9	Old Man	55

Dan 12:3	Brightness	55
Dan 7:10	Judgment Day	62
Dan 8:3	A Ram	22
Dan 8:6-7	Ram Destroyed	27
Dan 9:24	Eternal Righteousness	20
Dan 11:38	The female Power	23
Deut 1:30	He Shall Fight For You	9
Deut 25:5	Levirite Marriage	25
Deut 30:15-18	Life & Good	44
Deut 32:17	Sacrifices	28
Deut 4:24	Purifying Fire	78
Eph 1:7	Sins Forgiven	69
Eph 3:16	Inner Man	12
Eph 4:11-12	Righteousness	65
Eph 4:13	God's Power	4
Ex 12:41	Hosts Of The Lord	76
Ex 13:21	Pillar Of Fire	78
Ex 16:15	What Is It?	15
Ex 2:10	Living Water	82
Ex 2:23	Slavery	61
Ex 20:3	No other Gods	2
Ex 23:20-21	Protective Angel	68
Ex 23:22	Enemy To Your Enemies	69
Ex 3:2	Burning Bush	78
Ex 32:33	Sin Against Jehovah	62
Ezek 1:7	Body To Cart	5
Ezek 13:18	Witchcraft	74
Ezek 23:37	Idolatry	38
Ezek 9:4	The Mark of God	18
Ezek 9:4	The Mind of God	49
Gal 6:7	Sowing & Reaping	42
Gal 3:16	One Seed	41
Gen 1:1	Heaven & Earth	13
Gen 1:9	Dry Land	48
Gen 1:12-13	Third Day	24
Gen 15:5	Seed As The Stars	41
Gen 2:18	Help Meet	45
Gen 2:7	Shaped	15
Gen 20:2	Wife and Sister	81
Gen 28:12	Ladder To Heaven	11
Gen 28:14-15	Seed As The Dust	41
Gen 3:14-15	The Serpent	6
Gen 3:5	Like God	59
Gen 3:7	Eyes Opened	58

Reference	Title	Page
Gen 37:28	Joseph Sold	61
Gen 4:10	Abel's Blood	52
Gen 4:1-2	Cain & Abel	6
Gen 4:3-4	The Lord Accepts Abel	16
Gen 4:7	Sin Behind The Door	71
Gen 4:8	Abel Slain	52
Gen 6:5	Wicked Maturity	32
Heb 10:32	Gazingstock	27
Heb 11:4	Abel's Sacrifice	52
Heb 12:1	Easily Beset	43
Heb 13:8	Our Altar	21
Heb 3:1	High Priest	21
Heb 4:12	A Broken Neck	17
Heb 4:12	Soul From Spirit	79
Heb 4:14	Into The Heavens	21
Hos 10:12-13	Mercy Or Iniquity	42
Hos 14:2-3	Sin No More	61
Hos 8:7	Wind & Whirlwind	42
Is 11:11-12	A Second Time	36
Isa 25:8	Death Swallowed Up	62
Isa 27:1	Spiritual Sword	37
Isa 42:20	Blind To Sin	31a
Isa 62:4-5	Married	41
Isa 9:5	A Child Is Born	13
Isa 9:6-7	Government Of God	48
Jer 17:10	Heart & Reins	66
Jer 17:9	Deceitful Heart	67
Jer 20:9	Fire In My Bones	61
Job 1:9-11	On Trial	37
Job 1:12	In Satan's Power	42
Job 38:7	Morning Stars	55
Job 40:15	Behemoth	35
John 1:14	Spiritual Flesh	16
John 1:29	Lamb Of God	61
John 1:30	One Soul	11
John 1:36	Christ Jesus Is The Lamb	22
John 4:11	Living Water	14
John 5:36	God-Motivated Behavior	49
John 5:37	Mind Shaped	19
John 6:58	Heavenly Manna	15
John 7:38	Rivers Of Living Water	14
John 9:5	Jesus, Light Of The World	14
Josh 6:20	Naked	75
Lam 4:3	Cruel as the Ostrich	33

Reference	Topic	Page
Luke 1:67	The Soul Of Abel In Men	52
Luke 14:29	Foundation	6
Matt 8:20	No Pillow	13
Matt 11:14	Elias	20
Matt 13:24	Seed	10
Num 12:1-2	Moses' Marriage	51
Num 13:17	Spy Out The Land	73
Num 13:28-29	Inhabitants Of The Land	73
Num 21:6	Fiery Serpents	5
Phil 2:5	Another Mind	45
Phil 3:14	Mark of God	18
Phil 3:20	Heavenly Citizenship	49
Prov 2:9	Understanding	65
Prov 22:15	Foolish Youth	32
Prov 23:32	A Serpent's Bite	53
Prov 3:3	Tables Of The Heart	63
Ps 12:6	Pure Words	63
Ps 17:13	The Lash	37
Ps 42:1	A Female Deer	11
Ps 44:21-22	Secrets Of The Heart	65
Ps 68:22	I Will Fetch Them	22
Ps 68:31	Rod Of Correction	61
Ps 69:28	In The Book	63
Ps 73:6-9	Words Of Pride	30
Ps 82:6-7	Ye Shall Die Like Men	60
Rev 12:4-5	A Male Child	12
Rev 12:11	Blood Of The Lamb	22
Rev 14:4	Virgins	61
Rev 17:16	Burnt With Fire	61
Rev 19:7	The Lamb's Wife	22
Rev 2:17	Hidden Manna	15
Rev 20:12	According To Their Works	62
Rev 20:12	Books Opened	66
Rev 4:7	A Spiritual Calf Mind	11
Rev 4:7	New Testament Calf	22
Rev 6:9	Under The Altar	21
Rev 7:17	Lamb In The Midst	22
Rom 1:28	Reprobate Mind	6
Rom 11:26	All Israel Saved	36
Rom 13:1	No Power, But God	23
Rom 13:11	Awake Out Of Sleep	6
Rom 5:11	The Atonement	61
Rom 6:23	Wages Of Sin	62
Rom 6:6	Body Of Sin	55

Rom 7:23	Warlike Powers	27
Rom 7:4	Spiritual Husband	8
Rom 7:4	Married to Christ	12
Rom 8:7	Carnal Mind	6
Song 2:9	Behind The Wall	82
Song 4:10	Sister and Bride	81
Song 5:4, 6	Seduction & Ruin	26
Zech 3:2	Satan Rebuked	43

Sorted By Title

Title	Scripture	Note
A Broken Neck	Heb 4:12	17
A Child Is Born	Isa 9:5	13
A Female Deer	Ps 42:1	11
A Male Child	Rev 12:4-5	12
A Parable Of The Seeds	--------------	16
A Ram	Dan 8:3	22
A Second Time	Is 11:11-12	36
A Serpent's Bite	Prov 23:32	53
A Spiritual Calf Mind	Rev 4:7	11
Abel Slain	Gen 4:8	52
Abel's Blood	Gen 4:10	52
Abel's Sacrifice	Heb 11:4	52
According To Their Works	Rev 20:12	62
All Israel Saved	Rom 11:26	36
Another Heart	1 Sam 10:9	45
Another Mind	Phil 2:5	45
Atonement	Rom 5:11	61
Awake Out Of Sleep	Rom 13:11	6
Awake To Righteousness	1 Cor 15:34	6
Behemoth	Job 40:15	35
Behind The Wall	Song 2:9	75
Bitten	Acts 7:54	53
Blind To Sin	Isa 42:20	31a
Blinded Eyes	1 John 2:11	31a
Blinded Minds	2 Cor 4:4	31a
Blood Of The Lamb	Rev 12:11	22
Body Of Sin	Rom 6:6	55
Body To Cart	Ezek 1:7	5
Books Opened	Rev 20:12	66
Brightness	Dan 12:3	55
Burning Bush	Ex 3:2	78
Burnt With Fire	Rev 17:16	61
Cain & Abel	Gen 4:1-2	6
Carnal Mind	Rom 8:7	6
Christ Jesus Is The Lamb	John 1:36	22
Complete	Col 2:10	26
Cruel as the Ostrich	Lam 4:3	33

Death Swallowed Up	Isa 25:8	62
Deceitful Heart	Jer 17:9	67
Dishonesty	2 Cor 4:2	32
Dry Land	Gen 1:9	48
Easily Beset	Heb 12:1	43
Elias	Matt 11:14	20
Elymas	Acts 13:8	26
Enemy To Your Enemies	Ex 23:22	69
Eternal Righteousness	Dan 9:24	20
Eyes Opened	Gen 3:7	58
Female Power	Dan 11:38	23
Fiery Serpents	Num 21:6	5
Fire In My Bones	Jer 20:9	61
Foolish Youth	Prov 22:15	32
Foolishness Of Preaching	1 Cor 1:21	16
Foundation	Luke 14:29	6
Gazingstock	Heb 10:32	26
God's Power	1 Kings 19:13	4
God's Power	Eph 4:13	4
God-Motivated Behavior	John 5:36	49
Government Of God	Isa 9:6-7	48
Harvest	2 Sam 24:21-23	79
He Shall Fight For You	Deut 1:30	9
Heart & Reins	Jer 17:10	66
Heaven & Earth	Gen 1:1	13
Heavenly Citizenship	Phil 3:20	49
Heavenly Manna	John 6:58	15
Help Meet	Gen 2:18	45
Hidden Darkness	1 Cor 4:5	67
Hidden Manna	Rev 2:17	18
High Priest	Heb 3:1	21
Hosts Of The Lord	Ex 12:41	76
I Will Fetch Them	Ps 68:22	22
Idolatry	Ezek 23:37	38
Idolatry In Israel	2 Kings 18:4	2
In The Cloud	1 Cor 10:2-4	8
In Satan's Power	Job 1:12	42
In The Book	Ps 69:28	63
Inhabitants Of The Land	Num 13:28-29	73
Inner Man	Eph 3:16	12
Into The Heavens	Heb 4:14	21
Jeroboam	1 Kings 12:26-29	31b
Jesus, Light Of The World	John 9:5	14
Joseph Sold	Gen 37:28	61

Judgment Day	Dan 7:10	62
Justice	1 Kings 3:28	74
Ladder To Heaven	Gen 28:12	11
Lamb In The Midst	Rev 7:17	22
Lamb Of God	John 1:29	61
Lamb's Wife	Rev 19:7	22
Lash	Ps 17:13	37
Levirite Marriage	Deut 25:5	25
Life & Good	Deut 30:15-18	44
Light Of The World	Matt 5:14	14
Like God	Gen 3:5	59
Living Water	John 4:11	14
Lord Accepts Abel	Gen 4:3-4	16
Mark Of God	Ezek 9:4	18
Mark of God	Phil 3:14	18
Married	Isa 62:4-5	41
Married to Christ	Rom 7:4	12
Mercy Or Iniquity	Hos 10:12-13	42
Mind Of God	Ezek 9:4	49
Mind Shaped	John 5:37	19
Money For Power	Acts 8:19-20	74
Morning Stars	Job 38:7	55
Moses' Marriage	Num 12:1-2	51
Naked	Josh 6:20	75
New Testament Calf	Rev 4:7	22
No Man Need Teach You	1 John 2:27	27
No other Gods	Ex 20:3	2
No Pillow	Matt 8:20	13
No Power, But God	Rom 13:1	23
Old Man	Col 3:9	55
One Seed	Gal 3:16	41
Only One Mediator	1 Tim 2:5	13
On Trial	Job 1:9-11	37
Our Altar	Heb 13:8	21
Passing The Love Of Women	2 Sam 1:26	12
Pillar Of Fire	Ex 13:21	78
Power Of God	Acts 1:8	48
Protective Angel	Ex 23:20-21	68
Pure Words	Ps 12:6	63
Purifying Fire	Deut 4:24	78
Ram Destroyed	Dan 8:6-7	27
Repentance	Acts 5:31	43
Reprobate Mind	Rom 1:28	6
Righteousness	Eph 4:11-12	65

Rivers Of Living Water	John 7:38	14
Rod Of Correction	Ps 68:31	61
Sacrifices	Deut 32:17	28
Satan Rebuked	Zech 3:2	43
Secrets Of The Heart	Ps 44:21-22	65
Seduction & Ruin	Song 5:4, 6	26
Seed	Matt 13:24	10
Seed As The Dust	Gen 28:14-15	41
Seed As The Stars	Gen 15:5	39
Serpent	Gen 3:14-15	6
Shaped	Gen 2:7	19
Sin Against Jehovah	Ex 32:33	62
Sin Behind The Door	Gen 4:7	71
Sin No More	Hos 14:2-3	61
Sins Forgiven	Eph 1:7	69
Sins Of The World	1 John 2:2	22
Sister and Bride	Song 4:10	81
Slavery	Ex 2:23	61
Sorcery	Acts 8:9	74
Soul From Spirit	Heb 4:12	79
Soul Of Abel In Men	Luke 1:67	52
Sowing & Reaping	Gal 6:7	42
Spiritual Altar	Heb 13:10	21
Spiritual Darkness	1 Cor 4:5	32
Spiritual Flesh	John 1:14	16
Spiritual Husband	Rom 7:4	8
Spiritual Sword	Isa 27:1	9
Spiritual Weapons	2 Cor 10:4	9
Spy Out The Land	Num 13:17	73
Sting Of Death	1 Cor 15:55	62
Tables Of The Heart	Prov 3:3	63
Third Day	1 Cor 15:4	24
Third Day	Gen 1:12-13	24
Under The Altar	Rev 6:9	21
Understanding	Prov 2:9	65
Uriah	2 Sam 12:9-10	16
Virgins	Rev 14:4	61
Wages Of Sin	Rom 6:23	62
Warlike Powers	Rom 7:23	27
Waters Divided	2 Kings 2:8	48
Waters Parted	2 Kings 2:14	48
What Is It?	Ex 16:15	15
Wicked Maturity	Gen 6:5	32
Wife and Sister	Gen 20:2	81

Wind & Whirlwind	Hos 8:7	42
Witchcraft	Ezek 13:18	74
Words Of Pride	Ps 73:6-9	30
Ye Shall Die Like Men	Ps 82:6-7	60

Soncino Zohar

Bemidbar, Section 3, Page 152a
  Adam Kadmon, Super-Soul 213
  Soul Of The Torah 212
Bemidbar, Section 3, Page 155b
  Bread Of Propagation 137
Bereshith, Section 1 Page 62a
  Neshamah 186
Bereshith, Section 1, Page 114a
  Adam Slain 142
Bereshith, Section 1, Page 12b
  Water Of The Torah 202
Bereshith, Section 1, Page 135b
  Well Of Existence 134
Bereshith, Section 1, Page 15b
  The Beginning 235
Bereshith, Section 1, Page 171a
  Idolatry & The Serpent 200
Bereshith, Section 1, Page 1b
  The Voice Of Tender Children 213
Bereshith, Section 1, Page 237b
  Metatron 124
Bereshith, Section 1, Page 4a
  A Female Deer 123
Bereshith, Section 1, Page 135b
  Angel Of The Covenant 219
Shemoth, Raya Mehemna, Page 43a
  Firstling Of An Ass 207
Shemoth, Section 2, Page 134b
  Take My Wife 233
Shemoth, Section 2, Page 135a
  Take My Wife 233
Shemoth, Section 2, Page 183b

Spiritual Bread 135
Shemoth, Section 2, Page 238a
    Moses Is Adam 229
Shemoth, Section 2, Page 90b
    Engraved Name Of The Holy One 213
Shemoth, Section 2, Page 95a
    Seeds Of Wisdom 202

Appendices

Appendix 1

The 10 Sefirot

Keter (Crown)

Chochmah (Father)

Binah (Mother)

Chesed (Loving Kindness)

Gevurah (Strength)

Tiferet (Justice – Perfect Balance)

Netzach (Drive To Succeed)

Hod (Self-Interest)

Yesod (Foundation)

Malchut (Female)

Appendix 2

The Keter

Every world consists of ten Sefirot. The first Sefirah of the ten is called, **Keter, the head**, but this **head** is actually three heads.

The first head of the Keter connects the other nine Sefirot of that world to the world above.

It is called **the unknowable head** because the nine Sefirot below, as well as the world above that it is attached to. are unaware of this head.

The second head is called, **Golgath, the skull**, which represents the will to create.

This head is the root of Messiah's soul.

The third head is called **the Concealed Brain**.

It is the hidden wisdom of God.

NEW TESTAMENT

The Lord Jesus Christ enclothes the Keter of Atzilut.

The one who was previously unknown to the world below is now known by everyone who is attached to him.

Acts 17:28

28 For in him we live, and move, and have our being; as certain also of your own poets have said, For we are also his offspring.

KJV

Appendix 3

Five Levels Of Soul

Nefesh is the animating life force in the blood.

Ruach is the breath, the oxygen in the blood.

Neshamah is the spiritual, intellectual soul of God.

Chayyah is the moral authority of God, which imparts *life* to the material body.

Yechida is *oneness*. The collective soul that comes from God.

Everyone born of a woman has a nefesh and a ruach.

The three other aspects of soul are *given*, according to the Will of God.

Appendix 4

Soul Universes

Beriah, The World of Creation.

Yetzirah, The World of Forms (sometimes called *The Astral Plane*).

Asiyah, the World of Action, which is this visible world.

Atzilut, the World of Emanation, is an aspect of *The World of Rectification*, which is a *universe of mind.* (See Appendix 5.)

The World of Atzilut functions as a channel through which God accesses *the soul universes* and communicates with the personalities of humanity that reveal him in the visible world.

Appendix 5
The Primeval Worlds

Kabbalah teaches that there are three spiritual worlds, or spiritual universes.

Two are primeval and the third is a correction of the second, which was destroyed.

These three worlds are not a part of the three *soul universes* described in Appendix 4.

They are *universes of mind.* They do not contain any aspect of soul.

The *perfected soul universe* will, however, contain an aspect of the *World of Rectification,* which is mind.

The World of Bound Lights (Akudim) is the first world to come into existence.

The World of Bound Lights is made from the breath that Jehovah breathed into the man.

The World of Points (Nekudim) is the second world to come into existence.

The World of Points is formed by the first light of creation.

According to Rabbi Luria's Kabbalah, *The World of Points* emerged out of *The World of Bound Lights,* and was destroyed.

The Word of Rectification (Berudim) is the third world to come into existence.

The World of Rectification is the reconstructed *World of Points*, which was destroyed.

The World of Atzilut is the personal name for *The World of Rectification*

The World of Atzilut is an intermediary channel between the soul worlds and the World of Adam Kadmon, primordial human.

All of these worlds are represented as concentric circles, each one inside of another.

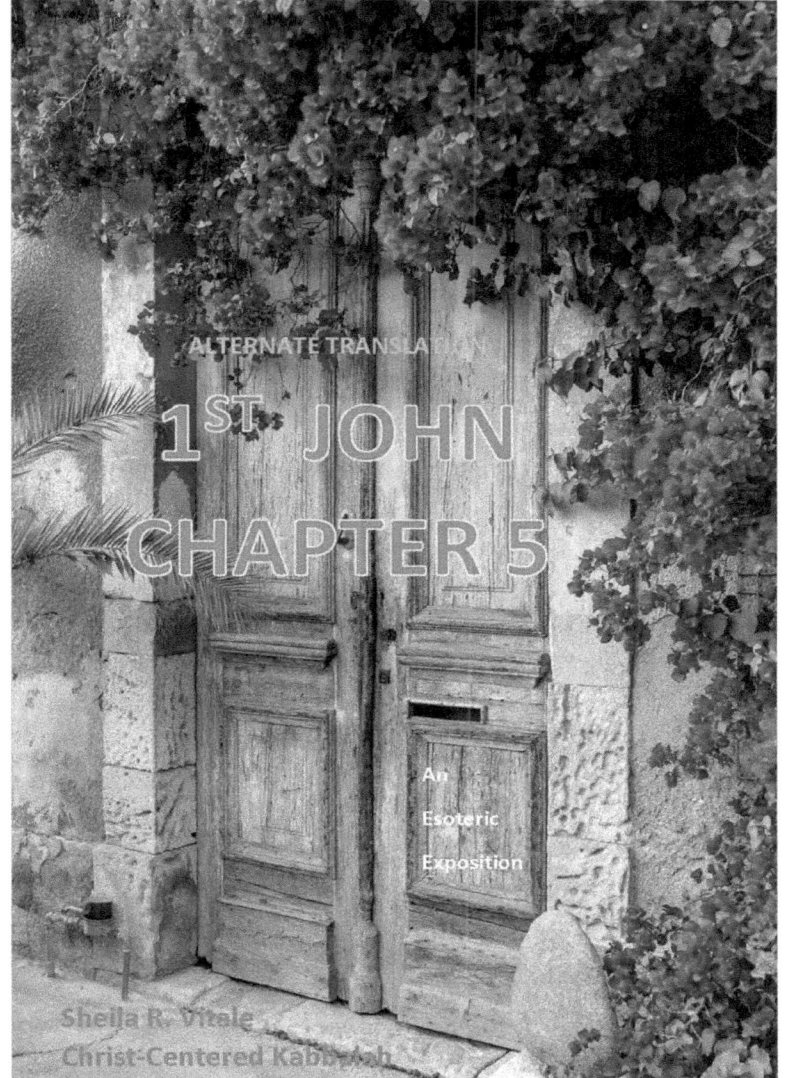

The Kabbalah of
The First Epistle of John
Chapter 5

An Esoteric Exposition
The Alternate Translation Bible (ATB)

Sheila Vitale
Christ-Centered Kabbalah

SOPHIA
EXPERIENCING 2ND THESSALONIANS, CHAPTER 2

SHEILA R. VITALE

LIVING EPISTLES MINISTRIES

The Noah Chronicles

An Esoteric Exposition of Noah's Seduction

Including the Alternate Translation of
Genesis 9:18-27

Sheila R. Vitale

Christ-Centered Kabbalah

THE COMMON SALVATION

The Book of Jude Unlocked Through Kabbalah

Sheila R. Vitale
Christ-Centered Kabbalah

About The Author

SHEILA R. VITALE

Sheila R. Vitale is the Spiritual Leader, Founding Teacher and Pastor of <u>Christ-Centered Kabbalah (CCK)</u>. Pastor Vitale has been expounding upon the Torah (Scripture) through a unique Judeo-Christian lens for nearly three decades, and has an international following. As head of the teaching ministries, she disseminates Judeo-Christian literature, both printed and online, to individuals around the world.

In addition to managing CCK, Pastor Vitale is an illustrator of spiritual principles, researcher, translator, social commentator, lecturer, movie, TV and theater critic, and author. She has given more than 1,000 *LEM* lectures that explain hundreds of spiritual principles, all of which may be purchased on CDs or as downloadable MP3s. In addition, beginning in the year 2013, Videos of Pastor Vitale's lectures became available for purchase on DVDs or downloadable MP4s.

She has written more than 40 books based upon the Old and New Testaments and authentic Rabbinic Kabbalah, including *The Noah Chronicles, The Crime of the Calf* and *The Doctrine of the Ox*, as well as unique and esoteric translations of canonical Biblical texts such as *The Prophesies of Daniel, Chapter 8*, <u>*The Prophesies of Daniel According to Kabbalah, Chapter 11*</u>, *Sophia* and *The Common Salvation*. Other publications include, *1 Corinthians, Chapter 11* and *Unconscious Mind Control*.

KABBALAH AND CHRIST-CENTERED KABBALAH

Pastor Vitale has been studying Torah (Scripture) and the New Testament, in-depth, since the 1970s, and began to teach her understanding of it, which she calls The Doctrine of Christ, in January of 1988. In the year 2000, she began to study and teach the Jewish spiritual philosophy of authentic *Lurian Kabbalah*. Since then, she has woven her continuously evolving understanding of *The Doctrine of Christ* and *Lurian Kabbalah* into a fascinating and unparalleled course of study that she calls, *Christ-Centered Kabbalah*.

Christ-centered Kabbalah, the union of the two systems, is more than one + one = two. The integration of the two philosophies has produced a new, vigorous approach to spiritual ascension (rectification) which offers a fresh hope (both natural and spiritual) to all who wait for Israel to be restored to Adam's first estate, and to an even higher estate, one from which he will never fall down again.

Christ-Centered Kabbalah is based upon her original research in the Hebrew text of the Torah, the foundational books of *Philosophical Kabbalah*, such as *The Zohar*, and the Greek text of *The New Testament*. She was teaching *The Doctrine of Christ* with *Lurian Kabbalah* for at least one year when, in 2001, the Lord Jesus Christ divided the ministries and established Christ-*Centered Kabbalah*.

She has also been studying the authentic Jewish Kabbalah of several Rabbinic scholars, including *Moses Nachmanides* (Ramban), *Moses Cordovero (*Ramak*)* and *Isaac Luria (*The Ari*)* since the year 2000. She has read many of the English translations of their writings, including *Ramban's The Gate of Reward*, *Ramak's Pardes Rimonim (Orchard of Pomegranates*), and *The* teachings *of the Ari*, as written by his student, *Chayyim Vital*, in *The Tree of Life: The Palace of Adam Kadmon*, and *The Gate of Reincarnations*.

She received the call to study *kosher* Jewish Kabbalah in August of the year 2000 while evangelizing in Greenville, South

Carolina. At that time, the Spirit of God directed her to read and study the teachings of Rabbi Luria, as written by his student, *Chayyim Vital,* in *The Tree of Life: The Palace of Adam Kadmon.* She could not understand it, but continued to read anyway. Shortly thereafter, she saw an angel enter into her, and the eyes of her understanding began to open. Pastor Vitale attributes her ability to understand and teach authentic Jewish Kabbalah and *Christ-Centered Kabbalah,* which she believes is beyond the grasp of the human mind, to the Lord Jesus Christ.

She often cautions her students about the dangers of Qabalah that is not kosher. She asks everyone who would like to know more about her to please note that all Kabbalah is not kosher (authentic). Pastor Vitale teaches *authentic Kabbalah, which glorifies God*, and she shuns the *occult Qabalah* of personal power, which, all too frequently, is used to control unsuspecting persons, acquire wealth by spiritual power, or punish one's enemies.

She continues today to manage *Christ-Centered Kabbalah* and to write and teach about *authentic Kabbalah and Christ-Centered Kabbalah.*

BEGINNINGS, INSPIRATION AND CALLING

Sheila Vitale was born into a Jewish family, and began her spiritual journey as a child when her mother enrolled her as a student in an Orthodox Hebrew school. She also attended synagogue on Shabbat during that time, where she experienced the Spirit of God for the first time. Such a deep longing for God was stirred up in her that she wept. She was touched so profoundly that she became desperate to attend yeshiva (Jewish high school) but her parents could not afford to send her.

She became very ill around the age of 11, and has battled with chronic illness ever since. (Her most recent struggle against premature death came in 1990, when she spent three months in the hospital.) Her illnesses led her to cry out to God, seeking a deeper understanding of what was happening to her.

Much later, as an adult, after years of searching, she, once again, experienced the Spirit that had brought her to tears, but this time it was in *Gospel Revivals Ministries*, a Pentecostal church where Deliverance Ministry was emphasized. She had desired a deeper understanding of Scripture since her early years, so she began to attend church regularly. She read at least one Chapter of the Bible every day, but did not understand what she was reading. Scripture was difficult for her, and she struggled with the task. After about six months, however, while reading the Bible, she saw a vision of the angel with the little book described in Chapter 10 of the Book of Revelation, Verse 8. She began to understand the Bible after that, but several more years had to pass before she began to receive Revelation knowledge of the Scripture.

Sheila Vitale studied the Bible and Deliverance Ministry for about seven years under the teaching of *Charles Holzhauser*, the Pastor of *Gospel Revivals Ministries*, in Mount Sinai, NY. Sometimes she attended as many as five teaching services each week, as well as studying for endless hours to gain key insight into her faith. She also edited *Pastor Holzhauser's* books during that time. After that, she studied independently under the influence and direction of the Holy Spirit, before founding *Living Epistles Ministries (LEM)*.

She began to learn authentic *Lurian Kabbalah* in October of 2000 and to teach it in 2001. After that, in November of 2002, she began to teach Kabbalah creatively. Thus, after serving 12 years with *LEM*, she undertook a second mission and founded *Christ-Centered Kabbalah*, which emerged as a vehicle for the publishing and distribution of her unique brand of Kabbalah.

WRITINGS AND WORK TODAY

Sheila Vitale's signature work is the three volumes of *The Alternate Translation Bible*: *The Alternate Translation Of The Old Testament, The Alternate Translation of the New Testament* and *The Alternate Translation of the Book of Revelation*. *The Alternate Translation Bible* is an esoteric translation of the Scripture, and is not intended to replace traditional translations.

The Book of Revelation and several other books that Pastor Vitale has written have been translated into Spanish.

She is currently submitting *CCK* books for retail sale through *Barnes & Noble*. Paperback and digital versions of the books are also available at Amazon.com and the official *CCK* website. She also has an *Author's* website which displays all of her books, as well as several photographs of her and a short bio. She also writes for the *Blog* on the CCK website, where a detailed review of radio talk show host, Alex Jones', interview of Louis Farrakhan is posted. She has also delivered hundreds of messages, many of which have been transcribed and may be viewed free of charge on the *Christ-Centered Kabbalah* website.

She also continues to publish and make a wide range of Biblical translations and educational materials available for free on the *CCK* official website, as well as providing free video lectures to the public through *the Christ-Centered Kabbalah YouTube channel*. She also has another YouTube channel called *Short Clip by Sheila R. Vitale,* where she posts short, focused messages which average 15 minutes each.

PASTOR VITALE TODAY

Sheila Vitale serves a range of ecclesiastical, educational, and administrative functions from her headquarters in Port Jefferson Station, New York. Operating in the Offices of Evangelist, Prophet, Teacher of Apostolic Doctrine and Pastor, she continues delivering her powerful messages on a range of topics, from movie reviews and social commentaries to esoteric interpretations of the Scripture, Torah, Messiah, Noah, Judgment, Science, Ascension, Immortality and Reincarnation and Pagan & Judeo-Christian Spiritual Roots.

She has dedicated her life to studying and teaching Judeo-Christian spiritual principles, and continues to focus daily on studying, teaching and writing. In February of 2016, she joined other *CCK* teachers to dedicate a new *CCK* Building in Gray Court, South Carolina.

She is also a philanthropic individual who supports numerous charitable organizations, including *Feed the Children,*

Judicial Watch, *World Vision*, *Lighthouse Mission*, and *The International Fellowship of Christians and Jews*. She also helps local groups such as the *Terryville Fire Department*. In her spare time, Pastor Vitale enjoys watching movies, attending plays and partaking of cuisines from different cultures. An avid traveler, she has visited numerous countries in Europe and Africa as well as many cities in the United States.

Christ-Centered Kabbalah
Sheila R Vitale,
Pastor, Teacher & Founder
~ The Compleat Kabbalah ~
PO Box 562, Port Jefferson Station, New York 11776, USA
Christ-CenteredKabbalah.org *or* Books@Christ-CenteredKabbalah.org
(631) 331-1493

www.ingramcontent.com/pod-product-compliance
Lightning Source LLC
Chambersburg PA
CBHW071315150426
43191CB00007B/627